# THE JOURNAL OF A
# TOUR TO CORSICA;
# AND MEMOIRS OF
# PASCAL PAOLI

Hôtel "Les EUCALYPTUS"
20140 PORTO POLLO
Tél. 04 95 74 01 52
SIRET : 408 020 352 00014
Email : portopollo@hotmail.com

On the trail of James Boswell,
July 2007.

JAMES BOSWELL IN ROME, MAY, 1765
From the oil painting by George Willison
(*By courtesy of the Scottish National Portrait Gallery*)

# THE JOURNAL OF A TOUR TO CORSICA; AND MEMOIRS OF PASCAL PAOLI

## BY JAMES BOSWELL, ESQ.

Olim meminisse juvabit.  VIRG.  [*Æneid* I, 203]

T U R T L E   P O I N T   P R E S S

*103 Hog Hill Road, Chappaqua, New York 10514*

# BIBLIOGRAPHICAL NOTE

THE text used for this edition is that of the first edition of 1768, collated with that of the third edition of 1769; and, following the example of my judicious predecessors, I have made no attempt to emend the occasional characteristic liberties that Boswell has taken with the French and Italian languages.

Grateful acknowledgement is hereby made for permission to cite sundry passages included in the *Introduction* from various of the authorities listed hereunder; and, in especial, to the Oxford University Press, whose courtesy in allowing me to draw largely upon their invaluable edition of Boswell's *Letters* I greatly appreciate.

### Works Consulted for the Introduction

*Abbott.* A catalogue of papers relating to Boswell, Johnson and Sir William Forbes found at Fettercairn House a residence of the Rt. Hon. Lord Clinton, 1930–31. By Claude Colleer Abbott. 1936.

*Letters.* Letters of James Boswell. Collected and edited by Chauncey Brewster Tinker. 2v. 1924.

*Lewis.* The Hooded Hawk. By D. B. Wyndham Lewis. 1946.

*Life.* The Life of Samuel Johnson, LL.D. By James Boswell. Globe Edn. Edited by Mowbray Morris. 1914.

*Mallory.* Boswell the Biographer. By George Mallory. 1912.

*Roberts.* Journal of a Tour to Corsica. By James Boswell. Edited by S. C. Roberts. 1923.

*Scott.* The Portrait of Zélide. By Geoffrey Scott. 1925.

*Southey.* The Life of Horatio, Lord Nelson. By Robert Southey. Edited by Emma Gollancz. 1896.

*Tinker.* Young Boswell. By Chauncey Brewster Tinker. 1922.

## A Note on the Frontispiece

*It is tempting to conjecture that Boswell is here depicted in the very " scarlet and gold " to which allusion is made on page 122 of the following text, since his waistcoat and breeches are a reddish-pink with golden embroidery and garters. The fur-trimmed gown is olive-green ; and the owl seated above his head is, doubtless, Minerva's, typifying Wisdom.*

*The painter, Willison, was a Scotsman who studied in Rome, whence he returned in 1771, to settle in Greek Street, Soho. He exhibited at the Royal Academy for some years, but, meeting with no great success, he departed for the East Indies, where, apparently more by his knowledge of physic than by his art, he made a fortune. He died in Edinburgh in 1795.*

# INTRODUCTION

ON Monday, May 16th, 1763, as all the world knows, the back-parlour of Mr. Thomas Davies's book-shop at No. 8 Russell Street, Covent Garden, became the scene of perhaps the most auspicious meeting in the history of English letters. Dr. Johnson was then already in his fifty-fourth year, while James Boswell was not yet twenty-three. Considering the appalling nature of the initial exchanges, the intimacy of this oddly assorted couple proceeded at a prodigious rate, with one further meeting in May, three in June (one very brief, " near Temple-bar, about one o'clock in the morning "), some twelve in July, and two more, in London, in August—with results which are set forth in the greatest of all biographies. And then, on Friday, August 5th, the pair set out for Colchester and Harwich, so that Johnson, with ineffable condescension, might see off, upon his educational journey to Utrecht, his young friend of less than three months standing.

It was not until February 1766 that Boswell returned to England, and in the interim his travels had been extensive : he had flirted desperately with his ' Zélide ', Belle de Zuylen ; he had held converse with the Earl Marischal, Lord Keith, with Rousseau, Voltaire and Wilkes ; he had visited any number of petty German courts ; he had written to Johnson from the tomb of Melanchthon ; he had inspected most of the antiquities of Italy ; and he had traversed the almost unknown island of Corsica, then in a state of endemic insurrection, and had become the friend of the patriot leader, General Paoli. He had, in short, during the space of two years and a half, successfully

7

transformed himself from a raw Scottish youth into an experienced and travelled man of the world; and, because he was James Boswell, he had, at the same time, in all essential particulars, not altered in the slightest. On his return to England, with his head full of Corsica, he had proceeded to write the book with which we are here concerned : *An Account of Corsica, The Journal of a Tour to that Island ; and Memoirs of Pascal Paoli*; and, in February 1768, this was published by Edward and Charles Dilly. It was, moreover, so successful that a second edition was called for in the June of the same year, and a third, slightly revised, in the year following.

Since then, oddly enough, the Journal of his tour has been but twice reissued: once, together with the very juvenile *Letters between Erskine and Boswell*, in 1879, under the editorship of Dr. Birkbeck Hill; and once in an edition published in 1923 by the Cambridge University Press with a most valuable introduction by that great contemporary Johnsonian, Mr. S. C. Roberts. This tale of comparative neglect, when we consider the innumerable editions of the *Life of Johnson* and the *Journal of a Tour to the Hebrides*, would seem strange, and would indeed seem to indicate that the Corsica book, unlike its successors, had little to recommend it, were it not that far better judges than the present writer have agreed with him in thinking quite otherwise. Writing from Brighton on September 9th, 1769, Johnson himself was at pains to assure Boswell that " your Journal is in a very high degree curious and delightful. . . . You express images which operated strongly upon yourself, and you have impressed them with great force upon your readers. I know not whether I could name any narrative by which curiosity is better excited, or better gratified." [1]    And

[1] *Life*, p. 197.

almost the latest biographer of Boswell, Mr. D. B. Wyndham Lewis, in his *The Hooded Hawk* (1946) has a similar
tribute to pay : " Why *The Journal* . . . is not better
known I cannot imagine.  It is an entirely delightful little
book ; gay, amusing, high-spirited, well-bred, unpreten-
tious, full of gobbets of shrewd observation and surprising
good sense, and refreshingly devoid of the conventional
sneers found in insular books of travel." [1]  If to this we
add that so highly sophisticated a person as Madame du
Deffand confessed herself " *extrêmement contente* " [2] with
the work, and that a later and somewhat unexpected
admirer of it was Napoleon Buonaparte,[3] it is pretty
obvious that some reason extraneous to the book's actual
merits must be found to explain the comparative obscurity
in which it has languished since its initial success ; and,
as is so often the case, it is Johnson's penetrating eye
that provides the clue.  In the same letter that I have
quoted above, he also wrote : " Your History is like
other histories. . . . There is between the history and the
journal that difference which there will always be found
between notions borrowed from without, and notions
generated within.  Your history was copied from books ;
your journal rose out of your own experience and
observation."

Now what this means is that Boswell, being but twenty-
seven years of age at the time when he was compiling
his book, was an extremely ambitious young man who, as
his Preface, hereafter printed, makes very clear, had most
laudable notions as to the seriousness of literary activity ;
with the result that he had produced a book that falls
into two entirely separate parts.  The first, " copied
from books ", is a formal history of the island of Corsica,
with an account of its geography, flora, fauna and so

[1] *Lewis*, p. 100.        [2] *Tinker*, p. 17.        [3] *Lewis*, p. 117.

forth, that does not make very stimulating reading
nowadays; the second, which is a history of what Boswell
himself did, is a very different matter.   And so, in the
present edition, while the *Dedication to Paoli* is retained,
and also the *Preface* in which the author sets forth his own
highly characteristic views upon the dignity of authorship,
the odd two hundred and sixty pages in which he dilates
upon the history of Corsica, that, as he quite honestly
tell us in his Preface, mainly derive from the two French
books by M.G.D.C. and by M. Jaussin Ancien Apoticaire
Major, have been omitted; while the precious pages of the
Tour, which are based upon his Journal written at the
time, are given in full.

The ruthlessness of this proceeding must not, however,
be taken as intending to cast any reflection upon the
accuracy or ability of Boswell's geographical and historical
survey of Corsica.   It was, and indeed still may be for
all I know to the contrary, as good an account of the
place as exists in English.   It has, in fact, been so
described by no less an authority than Sir G. O.
Trevelyan; [1]  and it was, as recently as March 1923,
similarly extolled in an article written by Leonard Whibley
for *Blackwood's Magazine*. [2]   But—and this is the point—
whereas the number of people nowadays who are interested
in Corsica as it was in the eighteenth century, and in the
vicissitudes of its inhabitants, are necessarily limited, the
name and number of those who are interested in anything
to do with James Boswell himself are legion, and they are
not diminishing.   Since his *Corsica* is the earliest example
we possess of the method which he was to employ with
such entire success in the two great books that followed
it, and since, for all his youth and lack of experience,
it is a book that is full of the happiest and most individual

[1] *Tinker*, p. 112.          [2] *Roberts*, p. viii.

touches, there is a great deal to be learnt about James Boswell from a perusal of his *Tour*. To do this to the fullest extent, it is necessary to take rather more than a cursory glance at what we now know from other sources both of the man who visited Corsica in 1765, and of the man who later, at Auchinleck, in 1767, was engaged in writing his account of it.

* * * * *

One of the master-keys to the comprehension of James Boswell is the fact that, in conjunction with a quite unusual volatility of disposition, he possessed also an inordinate desire to be respected, not so much by others as by himself, as a man of solid achievement and solid worth. As early as May 21st, 1763, five days after his first meeting with Johnson, we find him writing to his Scottish mentor, Sir David Dalrymple, with reference to his friend, the Revd. William Johnson Temple : " He is a sober and a grave man. Indeed I have a satisfaction to think, that I am most happy in such company, which is a proof that I am at bottom a sober and grave man myself." [1]

A month later, he confides to the same correspondent : " My great object is to attain a proper conduct in life. How sad will it be, if I turn no better than I am ; I have much vivacity, which leads me to dissipation and folly. . . . I have at bottom a melancholy cast ; which dissipation relieves by making me thoughtless. . . . Tell me . . . if years do not strengthen the mind, and make it less susceptible of being hurt ? and if having a rational object will not keep up my spirits ? " [2]

Five days after, he is arranging with his solicitor [3] for the maintenance, while he is abroad, of his first illegitimate son, Charles ; but within another fortnight he is again assuring Dalrymple that he looks upon obtaining the

---

[1] *Letters*, p. 10.   [2] *Ibid.*, p. 11.   [3] *Ibid.*, pp. 14–15.

friendship of so great and good a man as Johnson as one
of the most important events of his life. " I think better
of myself when in his company than at any other time.
His conversation rouses every generous principle, and
kindles every laudable desire. . . . Let me go where I
will, I shall meet with no man from whom I can receive
more real improvement." [1] On July 23rd, the note is
the same : Johnson has " assisted me to obtain peace of
mind. He has assisted me to become a rational *Christian*.
. . . When I return from abroad I hope I may easily
drop loose acquaintance. . . . When we are with good
men, whose opinions agree with ours, we are then more
firmly fixed." [2] A week later : " I hope to be rationally
happy at Utrecht." [3]

Now, of course, it is perfectly easy to put all this down
to hypocrisy, particularly when, at almost the same time,
on the very eve of his departure from England, we find
Boswell consulting Dalrymple as to whether he thinks the
receipt of letters from John Wilkes " could hurt me, and
whether it could be concealed ". The trouble is, as he so
rightly points out, such letters " would be a treasure for
the next generation ".[4]

Here already, at the age of twenty-three, we have the
quintessential Boswellian dilemma. It is important, God
knows, for a man to be " rationally happy "; it is equally,
perhaps even more important to lay up treasure " for the
next generation ", even if such treasure is of so combustible
a nature as letters from such an ambiguous character as
Wilkes. Poor Boswell ! it was the dilemma in which he
was to pass his life. Fortunate was it for him when he
was able to meet men who, like Johnson and like Pascal
Paoli, were treasure for the next generation, and were, at

[1] *Letters*, p. 24.  [2] *Ibid.*, pp. 29–30.
[3] *Ibid.*, p. 39.  [4] *Ibid.*, p. 41.

the same time, morally desirable companions. He can hardly be blamed if, in such a case, he sometimes sacrificed his own peace of mind to the great cause of benefiting posterity. Besides, the truth must be faced : sometimes it was not at all difficult to do so. The secret of Boswell's greatness resided in the chameleon-like quality of his mind; as his company was, so was he. It is to our lasting good-fortune that he was so constituted; and it was, after all, he who paid the price. For us now there is nothing but undivided gain.

\* \* \* \* \*

The processes which led Boswell to Corsica were largely fortuitous ones. When he departed for Utrecht his ostensible purpose was to study law in that city, where, from August to December at any rate, he " stood upon his guard and repelled dissipation ". [1] In this meritorious activity, no doubt his new friend Belle de Zuylen was of the greatest assistance, for, though she was not beautiful, she was charming and most intelligent—a charm and an intelligence that may still be savoured by all who read Geoffrey Scott's incomparable book about her, *The Portrait of Zélide*. Yet even Zélide could not keep the mercurial Boswell stationary for very long, and, in January 1764, he had moved off to Leyden; and later, in June, he proceeded with the Earl Marischal Lord Keith and the latter's adopted Turkish daughter, Emetulla, to Brunswick, to arrive in Berlin upon July 7th. He was still in Berlin at the end of August, and was writing to Andrew Mitchell, the British envoy to the Court of Prussia : " My father seems much against my going to Italy." [2] Lord Auchinleck's opposition was understandable. He had handsomely enough allowed his son

[1] *Letters*, p. 43.　　[2] *Ibid.*, pp. 55–6.

two hundred and forty pounds a year to enable him to get on with his legal studies; and now Boswell was quoting the Apostle Paul: " I must see Rome." " It would ", he added, " give me infinite pleasure. It would give me taste for a life-time, and I should go home to Auchinleck with serene contentment. I am the more confident in my request that I am no libertine, and have a moral certainty of suffering no harm in Italy." [1] More, he did not intend to travel there as a *Mi Lord anglois*, but merely as a scholar and a man of elegant curiosity; and he had been told that, in that character, one might live in Italy very reasonably. Would Mitchell, therefore, be so good as to intercede with his father? Berlin, he felt, had nothing further to teach him, and he was resolved to leave it within a fortnight, and to proceed by way of Mannheim and " one or two more of the German courts to Geneva ". And then, all at once, in a single phrase, out pops from the bag the quintessential Boswellian cat. His travelling-companion, Keith, was acquainted with Rousseau, and so, at Geneva: " I am there at the point from whence I may either steer to Italy or to France. I shall see Voltaire. I shall also see Switzerland and Rousseau. These two men are to me greater objects than most statues or pictures." [1]

By Sunday, September 30th, he had come as far as Wittemberg, and was thence inditing upon the tomb of Melanchthon his celebrated letter to Johnson, which he did not, however, dare to despatch for nearly thirteen years more, " lest he should appear at once too superstitious and too enthusiastick ". It was not until December that he reached Switzerland.

The mechanics of Boswell's meeting with Rousseau require a rather careful handling, for a certain measure of

[1] *Letters*, p. 56.

disingenuousness creeps into his account of it. He had
not, as in his *Tour* he suggests he had, a letter of recommendation from the Earl Marischal. Instead, when he
had, by December 3rd, found his way to the Val de
Travers, he sat down and despatched to the " wild
philosopher " an extremely ingenious epistle in which he
expressed, among many other things, his earnest desire to
make himself worthy to belong to a nation that had
produced a Fletcher of Saltoun and an Earl Marischal.
Keith, it would seem, had told him that Rousseau took a
great deal of interest in Fletcher of Saltoun. " I have ",
he said, " a presentiment that a noble friendship is to be
born this day."

Rousseau could not resist so wonderful a letter. Indeed,
no-one could have resisted so wonderful a letter; and,
when the pair met, Rousseau informed his admirer, among
a variety of other matters, of how he had been approached
by the Corsican patriots, and had been requested by them
to assist in the formulating of their laws. Boswell alleges
that already, before this meeting, he had formed the
project of visiting Corsica, and this may be so; though
when, shortly after, he wrote to Sir Alexander Dick,[1]
giving his future plans, together with a full itinerary, he
says nothing at all about it. And certainly, when this
historic encounter was concluded, Boswell's next pro-
ceedings, so far as they concerned the brave Corsicans,
were singularly dilatory. He visited Voltaire at Ferney;
and then he went on to Turin where he fell in with Wilkes,
who was in hot pursuit of his mistress, Gertrude Corradini,
who had fled to Bologna. To Wilkes he wrote at once,
suggesting an interview whereat they might indulge in a
discussion upon " the immateriality of the soul "; [2] and,
what with one thing and another, he had, by March, got

[1] *Letters*, p. 62.  [2] *Ibid.*, p. 69.

no nearer to Corsica than Naples, which he reached by way of Parma and Rome, and whence, upon the 16th of that month, he and Wilkes made the ascent of Vesuvius and peered into the crater. After that they parted, and Boswell proceeded to Rome, to study antiquities and also to write to Wilkes about his suggestion that he should become " a foreign minister ".[1] " In the course of our correspondence," he added, " you shall have the various schemes which I form for getting tollerably through this strange existence. If you would think justly of me, you must ever remember that I have a melancholy mind. That is the great principle in my composition." [2]

A further six months passed, during which our anti-quarian visited Terni, Venice, Mantua, Florence and Siena, in which last place he conducted a vigorous love-affair with that Porzia Sansedoni who, some years later, wrote from that city to say she was glad he still re-membered her, that for her part she lives quietly now and prefers friends to lovers, but that all the same she would be greatly pleased to receive his promised portrait.[3] Already, as early as that May, he had written to Rousseau that his tour of Italy was almost completed, that he had seen classic places and formed his taste "up to a point "; though his " conduct had not been so virtuous ". Still, " one must be patient ". He continued : " De là [Parma] j'irai à Gênes pour m'embarquer pour la France ; mais je suis déterminé d'aller premierrement en Corse, comme je vous ai dit à Motiers. Je vous supplie donc de m'envoyer d'abord, aux soins de Messieurs Vautier et Delarue, à Gênes, une lettre de recommendation ; et si vous avez des ordres de conséquence, fiez-vous à moi. Je ne saurrois m'empêcher de faire une visite à ces braves insulaires qui ont tant fait pour leur indépendance et qui

[1] *Letters*, p. 74.  [2] *Ibid.*, p. 75.  [3] *Abbott*, p. 119.

ont choisi M. Rousseau pour leur législateur. Si vous ne m'écrivez pas, je leur montrerai la petite lettre que j'ai reçu de vous à Genève, avec votre cachet, *Vitam impendere Vero*,[1] et je crois que cela me procurera un bienvenu. Il sera singulier si on me pende comme un espion. Si vous m'aimez donc, Monsieur, ne perdez pas un moment de m'écrire. Ceci est un projet trop romanesque pour que je puisse m'en passer. Je suis serieux." [2]

And, in reply to this letter (which in the text that follows he incorrectly dates April), he received Rousseau's reply of May 30th, which is given in full hereafter. At long last, by October, he had reached Leghorn, whence he set sail to Corsica. His subsequent adventures are related in his *Tour*; but, in order to understand the state of affairs which greeted him on his arrival, we had now better take a brief glance at the somewhat complicated condition of events which then obtained in that island.

\*    \*    \*    \*    \*

It is only to be expected that an island in the geographical situation of Corsica should have had to endure a destiny of conquest and oppression. The Carthaginians, the Romans, the Goths, the Saracens, had all, in their turn, after the frantic fashion of history, become masters of the land; and at a later date it had been a bone of contention between the Pope, the Genoese and the French. One would have thought that such a destiny would have cured the inhabitants of any very strong inclination for the ardours of nationalism, yet it was not so; and, though they had first fallen into the clutches of Genoa as early as the beginning of the fourteenth century, they had always stoutly resisted their invaders, and their history was one

---

[1] *Juvenal, Sat.*, iv, 91.    [2] *Letters*, pp. 77–8.

B

of almost unbroken alternation between subjugation and revolt.

To come to comparatively recent times, the popular uprising which Boswell had travelled especially to inspect had really started in 1729, and had, with a few pacific intervals, been in full swing ever since. In 1734 the leader of the Corsicans had been one Giafferi, whose colleague was a Signor Giacinto Paoli, the father of Boswell's general; and to this pair of leaders had addressed himself by letter, in 1736, that remarkable personage Theodore, Baron Newhoff of Westphalia, who had then modestly proposed his willingness to assist the Corsican cause, provided that they, in return, would be so good as to elect him their king. Strange to say, the ingenuous islanders eagerly agreed to this, and Theodore duly arrived in his new kingdom, clad in a dignified Turkish dress, and bringing with him money amounting to some one thousand zechins of Tunis, some arms and ammunition, and a great many magnificent promises.

He then proceeded from one beleaguered Genoese fortress to the next, with a telescope in his hand, through which he sagely and silently surveyed the scene; and he also contrived that large packets should continually be arriving for him from the continent, which, so he assured the trusting Corsicans, were messages to him from the various other crowned heads of Europe.

After some eight months of this, however, he noticed that his subjects were beginning to grow somewhat less enthusiastic, and so he departed to Holland, where he very cleverly obtained both credit and cannon from various merchants, mostly Jews, who permitted him to take back these articles with him to Corsica, together with a supercargo who was supposed to be in charge of them. When, in 1739, he reached his kingdom again, he at once dealt with the luckless supercargo by the simple method of having him put to death; but unhappily he found that, in the interim, the Genoese had called in the aid of the French. His essay in the workings of the credit-system thus proving to be of little avail, he was obliged to flee to England, where, after making over his kingdom as security to his creditors, he eventually expired in 1756, and was buried in the churchyard of St. Anne's, Soho, where a tablet may still be seen attesting his tribulations :

> The grave, great teacher, to a level brings,
> Heroes, and beggars, galley-slaves, and kings;
> But Theodore, this moral learn'd, e'er dead;
> Fate pour'd its lesson on his living head,
> Bestow'd a kingdom, and deny'd him bread.

As for the French, they had arrived upon the island in March 1738, and by the end of 1739 had succeeded in quelling the revolt. Giafferi and the elder Paoli fled to Naples, and their conquerors, being now otherwise occupied, by degrees withdrew their garrison, and in 1741 left the Genoese to get on with the business; whereat the Corsicans once again rose in arms. In 1745, Great Britain, in accordance with the political exigencies of the moment, bombarded the harbours of Bastia and San Fiorenzo, that were held by Genoa; and, though this was done more to inconvenience the Genoese than to benefit the Corsicans, the latter were extremely grateful, since it enabled them, in the confusion, to assume control of both places. And consequently, in 1746, they despatched a couple of envoys to His Britannic Majesty's ambassador at the Court of Turin, with the proposal that Corsica should put herself entirely under the protection of Britain, an offer that the British Government, at the time, did not see its way to accept.

In the meanwhile, the Genoese and the Corsicans went on fighting; and when, in 1753, Giafferi, the patriot leader, was assassinated, Pasquale Paoli, the second son of his old associate Giacinto Paoli, who was living in retirement at Naples, was sent for, and was ultimately, in 1755, at the age of twenty-nine, elected General of the kingdom. He at once issued a proclamation, and began an enquiry into the situation of the affairs of the country, which were in great confusion. " There was (says Boswell) no sub-ordination, no discipline, no money, hardly any arms and ammunition; and, what was worse than all, little union among the people." Paoli at once proceeded to alter all that. " His persuasion and example, had wonderful force; all ranks exerted themselves, in providing what was necessary for carrying on the war with spirit; whereby, in a short time, the Genoese were driven to the remotest corners of the island." Paoli, without delay, settled down to " civilize the manners of the Corsicans ", and all might have gone admirably had not the Genoese, in 1764, once again prevailed upon the French to fight their battles for them, by arranging a treaty that provided for the immediate despatch of six battalions of French troops to garrison the fortified towns of Corsica for the next four years.

" When this treaty was first known in Europe (writes Boswell), every noble heart was afflicted; for every body believed, that France was again determined to carry fire and sword into Corsica, and blast the hopes of the brave islanders." Even Rousseau thought so, and was correspon-dingly indignant; but he might have spared his indigna-tion, since the real situation was not quite so bad as he had feared. The fact was that the chief motive for the com-plaisance of the French was a little debt of some millions of livres which they owed the Genoese, and that they had found it inconvenient, for the moment, to pay. Con-sequently they offered troops instead, and the Genoese, remembering how formerly they had had their island pacified for them by foreign arms, concluded that the same thing was about to happen again. In this they erred. The French battalions were duly forwarded, at the end of 1764, under the command of the Count de Marboeuf; but they merely shut themselves up in the garrison towns of Bastia, San Fiorenzo, Calvi, Algagliola and Ajaccio, and made preparations to stay there as comfortably as they could until the four years were over and the debt to Genoa liquidated.

Naturally this suited the Corsicans very well, and they accordingly conducted themselves "with the greatest propriety" towards their nominal invaders : they summoned a general council, and, in effect, assured the French that, so long as they left the Corsicans alone, the Corsicans would not molest them. Genoa was the enemy, not France; and, as Genoa was leaving all the fighting to France, and France was not doing any fighting, "the warlike operations of Corsica were now suspended", and the island upon which Boswell landed was one that, though technically at war, was actually at peace.[1]

We may well imagine, having regard to Corsica's earlier offer to place its destinies in the hands of Britain, that the sudden and inexplicable arrival of a magnificent young Briton, bearing letters of introduction from no less a personage than Rousseau to the head of the Corsican state, must have been regarded, by the gallant Corsicans themselves, as an event of immense political significance. It was, of course, nothing of the sort; but the fact that the Corsicans chose so to regard it, and insisted on heaping upon Boswell honours that would have been suited to a plenipotentiary is, beyond question I think, the reason

[1] All the foregoing section is based upon Boswell's own *Account of Corsica*.

why, on his return to England, he did, as will soon be apparent, behave just like a plenipotentiary. This is generally ascribed to an excess of vanity on his part. I doubt if vanity was entirely responsible; I think it can more reasonably be put down to the workings of a rather uneasy conscience. The Corsicans had deemed him a man of importance, and had treated him accordingly; he had, albeit unwittingly, obtained this treatment under false pretences; and the least he could do, therefore, was to exert himself to the utmost on their behalf. And this, as we shall see, is precisely what he did.

\*     \*     \*     \*     \*

Boswell, together with his Swiss servant, landed at Centuri, on the extreme northern tip of the island, in the month of October 1765, and his movements thereafter are faithfully recorded in the *Tour*. He remained on Corsica well into November, and it is unnecessary to enlarge here upon his adventures. From start to finish his narrative has all the charm, the truth and the vividness which are so apparent in his two better-known books. The portrait he gives of Paoli is a first sketch in that art of hero-worship which is responsible for his great finished portrait of Johnson; and the picture which he gives of himself is engaging, endearing and characteristic. Incidents abound that bear the authentic Boswellian stamp : his interview with the hangman of Corsica; his ride through the chestnut woods; the idyllic episode of the Great Seal of the Kingdom; his harangue to the men of Bastelica; his remarkable success as a flute-player; his description of the guide Ambrosio, whom, once he had heard of his unusual powers as a marksman, Boswell, though " under no apprehension ", desired to march where " I might see him ".

One or two minor points may perhaps be made. It is very curious to observe how, already, the influence of Dr. Johnson was at work. Not only does Boswell relate to Paoli several of the characteristic anecdotes which had already been stored up for use hereafter in the *Life*, but he also, in one case at least, catches, whether consciously or otherwise, Johnson's very cadence and appropriates it for his own. In the house of Signor Antonetti at Morsiglia, he was struck by seeing a small copy from Raphael, of St. Michael and the Dragon. " There was ", he comments, " no necessity for its being well done. To see the thing at all was what surprised me."

On July 31st, 1763, Johnson had made his famous analogy between a woman preaching and a dog's walking on his hind legs : " It is not done well," he had said; " but you are surprised to find it done at all." [1]

One point more : it is always instructive to see both sides of a picture. Hereafter we can read Boswell's version of his first encounter with Paoli; in Fanny Burney's *Diary*, Paoli, one evening at Mrs. Thrale's, gives an account of the way in which the same event had appeared to him : " He came ", said he, " to my country, and he fetched me some letter of recommending him; but I was of the belief he might be an impostor and an espy; for I look away from him, and in a moment I look to him again, and I behold his tablets. Oh ! he was to the work of writing down all I say ! Indeed, I was angry. But soon I discover he was no impostor and no espy; and I only find I was myself the monster he had come to discern. Oh, [Boswell] is a very good man; I love him indeed; so cheerful ! so gay ! so pleasant ! but at the first, oh ! I was indeed angry." [2]

No wonder, as Boswell relates, did Paoli seem to him at

[1] *Life*, p. 159.          [2] *Tinker*, p. 111.

first " very reserved "; no wonder that for ten minutes
they walked backwards and forwards through the room,
hardly saying a word, while Paoli looked at him with a
steadfast, keen and penetrating eye. All in the end was
well, but perhaps for a few moments, at the sight of those
tablets, it had been touch and go. The thought that the
author of the *Life of Johnson* might have perished pre-
maturely, as a martyr to his art, is indeed an uncom-
fortable one.

\* \* \* \* \*

By December 1st, Boswell was back in Genoa, and
writing to reproach Wilkes for his silence; and by the
start of the new year he had reached Lyons, on his way to
Paris. From here he addressed himself to Rousseau, in a
letter which never reached its destination, since the
philosopher had left for London the day before it was
written :

" Illustre philosophe ! (it ran) . . . J'ai été cinq
semaines dans l'île. J'ai beaucoup vu ses habitants. Je
me suis informé de tout avec une attention dont vous ne
me croyiez pas capable. J'ai connu intiment le noble
général Paoli. J'ai des trésors à vous communiquer. Si
vous êtes encore autant affectionné aux braves insulaires
que vous l'étiez en écrivant au galant Buttafuoco,[1] vous
m'embrasserez avec enthousiasme. Vous oublierez tous
vos maux pendant bien des soirs. Je vous ai les plus
grandes obligations pour m'avoir envoyé en Corse. Ce
voyage m'a fait un bien merveilleux. Il m'a rendu
comme si toutes les vies de Plutarque fussent fondues dans
mon esprit. Paoli a donné une trempe a mon âme
qu'elle ne perdra jamais. Je ne suis plus ce tendre inquiet

---

[1] See notes in the text, pp. 52 and 113, for more about " the
gallant Buttafuoco ".

qui se plaignait dans le Val-de-Travers.   Je suis homme.
Je pense pour moi : vous me recréez . . ." [1]

I have left this letter, as well as its predecessor, in its
original tongue, since Boswell's French (like that of our
own Mr. Churchill) has the enormous merit of reading just
as clearly as English.

Immediately upon his return to London, Boswell took
up the cause of the Corsicans in earnest, and, addressing
himself to the highest possible authority, besought,
through a relative, an interview with the elder Pitt.   The
Prime Minister was evidently willing to grant one, because,
on February 19th, 1766, Boswell wrote to him direct, as
follows :

Sir,

I have the honour to receive your most obliging letter,
and can with difficulty restrain myself from paying you
compliments on the very genteel manner in which you are
pleased to treat me.   But I come from a people among
whom even the honest arts of insinuation are unknown.
However you may by political circumstances be in one
view a simple individual, yet, Sir, Mr. Pitt will always be
the prime minister of the brave, the secretary of freedom
and of spirit ; and I hope that I may with propriety talk
to him of the views of the illustrious Paoli.

Be that as it may, I shall very much value the honour
of being admitted to your acquaintance.   I am with the
highest esteem, Sir,

Your most obedient and
most humble servant,
JAMES  BOSWELL [2]

In response to this, Boswell was invited to call upon
Pitt, who was then residing at the Duke of Grafton's house

[1] *Letters*, p. 86.                    [2] *Ibid.*, pp. 87–8.

in Great Bond Street. He arrived attired in his full
Corsican dress, and he presented to the Prime Minister a
letter from Paoli. The great man " smiled, but received
him very graciously in his Pompous manner ".[1]

Nor was this all. The *London Chronicle* early in 1766
abounded with paragraphs, either written or inspired by
Boswell himself, which pressed the claims of the Corsicans,
and underlined the importance of Boswell's visit to them.
As early as January 3rd, a communication from Leghorn
had announced : " Nothing can be a greater proof of the
weak and desponding spirit of the Genoese than the
apprehensions which Mr. Boswell's tour to Corsica has
occasioned." [2] And a further letter, from Turin, dated
three days later, said : " We are in great hopes that from
what he (i.e. Mr. Boswell) has seen, he will be able to
undeceive his countrymen with regard to the Corsican
nation." [2]

Boswell's mother had died when he was in Paris on his
journey home, and he could not delay in London for long.
But already, by April, before he departed for Scotland, he
had evidently broached to Temple his intention of writing
the Corsica book, since Temple, who was then at Cambridge, had consulted Gray about it, and had received
from him the advice that the sooner it were published the
better.[3] By May, Boswell was back at Auchinleck; and
by October we have definite tidings that the great work
is well under way. His confidant was Sir Alexander
Dick, to whom he wrote : " I am going on with my
*Account of Corsica*, and I hope to make it a tollerable
book. . . . I would wish to have old Plutarch at Auchinleck for a month or two, were it probable that he would
condescend to assist me ; and indeed I imagine he would

[1] *Letters*, pp. 87–8.     [2] *Roberts*, p. xi.
[3] *Abbott*, p. 128.

not be averse to it ".[1]    And he added that he was delighted with Sir Alexander's notion of having a solemn
service performed for Paoli's benefit in the cathedral of
Durham, though it is likely that the " solemn service "
resolved itself into a matter of a few prayers.

*        *        *        *        *

And now, in the intervals of legal practice, and of other
things, the writing of the Corsica book was in full swing.
The young author took the greatest pains; he wrote to
Rivarola,[2] the Sardinian Consul at Leghorn, to the Revd.
Andrew Burnaby,[3] the chaplain of the British factory at
the same place, even to his old acquaintance, the Revd.
Robert Brown,[4] at Utrecht; and in each case his request
was the same—for accurate information.   By the March
of 1767, he was able to tell Temple that he was hoping to
finish the book during the vacation.[5]    His own life, mean-
time, had been filled with distractions : there had been,
once more, the Moffat woman, his dear infidel (" Can I
do better than keep a dear infidel for my hours of Paphian
bliss? "); [6] and there was the prospect of yet another
addition to his irregular family (" What a fellow am I ! ").
Besides, he was very far from well.   Yet, despite all, the
work went on, and soon he was able to report : " It
elevates my soul, and makes me *spernere humum*.   I shall
have it finished by June." [7]   And, in the very same letter
in which he makes this announcement, comes the first
mention of that elusive Miss Blair who was later to plague
him to such a degree.

Still, despite his many troubles, he was nearly as good
as his word.   By July the book was so far advanced that
he was able to send specimens of it to Edward Dilly,
the bookseller, who at once perceived he was on to a good

[1] *Letters*, p. 92.        [2] *Ibid.*, p. 95.        [3] *Abbott*, p. 26.
[4] *Ibid.*, p. 23.   [5] *Letters*, p. 103.   [6] *Ibid.*, p. 97.   [7] *Ibid.*, p. 109.

thing and agreed to publish it, and, what was more, to pay Boswell one hundred guineas for the copyright.[1] Moreover, Dilly agreed that the printing should be carried out by the Foulis's of Glasgow, under the author's immediate supervision; [2] and in August he wrote again to congratulate his enterprising client upon a little preliminary self-advertisement which he had managed to get inserted in the *London Chronicle*.[1] He advised that the same process should be applied to the *Public Advertiser*,[3] of which he was himself a proprietor; and this also was done. And finally, in November, Dilly very sagely laid down the condition that, when the one thousand copies of the printed sheets were despatched from Glasgow to London, by sea, they should travel in two batches of five hundred apiece, in separate ships, so as to minimise the risk of loss by storm and tempest.[3]

Boswell, in the interim, had again been attacking Lord Chatham, at Bath, telling him of his plans, and further urging upon him the claims of the Corsicans. His letter ended : " Could your Lordship find time to honour me now and then with a letter ? I have been told how favourably your Lordship has spoken of me. To correspond with a Paoli and with a Chatham is enough to keep a young man ever ardent in the pursuit of virtuous fame." [4]

And very soon now the proof-sheets of his book were flying far and wide : to Temple,[5] to Lord Hailes,[5] to Sir Alexander Dick,[6] to Christopher Wyvill, the rector of Black Notley in Essex.[7] Boswell was certainly not above seeking counsel from anyone who would give it him ; and when Lord Hailes returned some sheets with the observation that he had been " much entertained and

[1] *Abbott*, p. 43.   [2] *Letters*, pp. 118–9.
[3] *Abbott*, p. 44.   [4] *Letters*, p. 111.   [5] *Ibid.*, p. 113.
[6] *Ibid.*, p. 121.   [7] *Ibid.*, p. 129.

instructed ", the budding author burst into a paean of
gratification : " Is not this noble ? " [1] he wrote to Temple.
Perhaps the most curious of all his assistants is one of
whom we only learn by studying his *Preface*.  He had,
it seems, required some help with the verse-translations
of Seneca which he wanted to use, and so he had made
application, in the *London Chronicle*, for versions that
should be worthy of the occasion.  The palm was born
away by a certain Thomas Day, Esquire, of Berkshire, of
whom no more need be said here than that he was that
same Day as later became perhaps the most practical
Rousseauist of all time, and ended by writing that
admirable didactic treatise, *The History of Sandford and
Merton*.  Unfortunately, Mr. Day was then only nineteen
years of age, a little young for Boswell, and so they
probably did not meet.  It is a great pity.  The conjunction would have been an edifying one.

Meanwhile, as he wrote to Temple : " The proof-sheets
amuse me finely at breakfast.  I cannot help hoping for
some applause.  You will be kind enough to communicate
to me all that you hear, and to conceal from me all censure.
. . . The last part of my work, entitled the *Journal of a
Tour of Corsica* is, in my opinion, the most valuable." [2]
It is interesting to note that Boswell, also, knew very well
which was the best part of his book.  And now, moreover,
as publication drew nearer, and more and more of his
friends commended his work, Boswell's own hopes of
personal perfection rose higher.  " Temple," he wrote,
" I wish to be at last an uniform pretty man. . . . I am
always for fixing some period for my perfection as far as
possible.  Let it be when my *Account of Corsica* is published.  I shall then have a character which I must
support." [3]

<hr>

[1] *Letters*, p. 114.     [2] *Ibid.*, pp. 128–9.     [3] *Ibid.*, p. 137.

Not all his early critics, however, were as flattering as his friends had been. Baretti, in particular, as befitted an Italian, had adjured him not to allow his admiration for the Corsicans to lead him into strictures upon Genoa, the most cultured city of Italy, whose citizens had been grossly maligned.[1] But Baretti was prejudiced, and Boswell had never liked him. Consequently he took no notice, and, when his book appeared, Baretti wrote to him again, and had the satisfaction of informing him that his Corsican friends were " no better than bloody-minded savages ".[1]

Boswell did not mind. No sooner was the book out than it was receiving praise from all quarters. Lord Lyttelton provided him with a panegyric that pleased him so well that he included it bodily in his third, revised, edition; and Horace Walpole, and Mrs. Macaulay, and Garrick wrote him what he himself called " noble letters ".[2] Mrs. Barbauld even broke into verse on his behalf, and produced a poem on Corsica in which she sang

> The working thoughts which swelled the breast
> Of generous Boswell.[3]

Two Dutch translations were soon going ahead; Zélide was talking of doing a French version, though the French version, when it came, was not after all from her hand;[4] and the book also appeared in German and Italian.[5] There is, indeed, as late as 1770, a letter which refers to a Russian translation[6] too, that was, however, interrupted, and perhaps finally, by the death of its translator. When one reflects that, so far as I am aware, it has never yet appeared worth any foreigner's while to translate[5] the Life of Johnson, it becomes clear that Boswell had really pulled off a triumph. His letters to Temple of this

---

[1] Abbott, p. 4.  [2] Letters, p. 147.  [3] Roberts, p. xii.
[4] Letters, p. 147.  [5] Mallory, p. 61.  [6] Abbott, p. 112.

period, though still full of his pre-matrimonial troubles and of laments for his " wildness ", show how pleased he was at his success. " Be assured that I shall never again behave in a manner so unworthy the friend of Paoli. . . . You cannot imagine how happy I am at your approbation." [1]

*       *       *       *       *

However, it was not, even at the start, all approbation. Horace Walpole, despite his allegedly " noble " letter to the author, was soon writing, not so amiably, to his friend Gray : " Pray read the new account of Corsica; what relates to Paoli will amuse you much. The author, Boswell, is a strange being, and . . . has a rage for knowing anybody that was ever talked of. He forced himself upon me in spite of my teeth and my doors, and I see he has given a foolish account of all he could pick up from me. . . . He then took an antipathy to me on Rousseau's account, abused me in the newspapers, and expected Rousseau to do so too; but as he came to see me no more, I forgave him the rest." [2]

Gray himself, a few days later, replied in the following, for him, singularly obtuse strain, similar to that adopted, years later, by Macaulay : " Mr. Boswell's book . . . has pleased and moved me strangely, all (I mean) that relates to Paoli. He is a man born two thousand years after his time ! The pamphlet proves what I have always maintained, that any fool may write a most valuable book by chance, if he will only tell us what he heard and saw with veracity. Of Mr. Boswell's truth I have not the least suspicion, because I am sure he could invent nothing of this kind. The true title of this part of the work is, a Dialogue between a Green-Goose and a Hero." [3]

[1] *Letters*, p. 153.   [2] *Tinker*, p. 63.   [3] *Letters*, p. 129 (footnote).

Lord Auchinleck, on the other hand, merely remarked that Jamie had " ta'en a toot on a new horn ";[1] but it was, I am sorry to say, Johnson's comment that was both the most crushing and the least forgivable. Barely a month after publication, he sent to the proud author a letter that is well known but must nevertheless be given here, if only that it may explain Boswell's surely dignified and courteous rejoinder :

My dear Boswell,

I have omitted a long time to write to you, without knowing very well why. I could not [2] tell why I should not write; for who would write to men who publish the letters of their friends, without their leave? Yet I write to you in spite of my caution, to tell you that I shall be glad to see you, and that I wish you would empty your head of Corsica, which I think has filled it rather too long. But, at all events, I shall be glad, very glad, to see you. I am, Sir, yours affectionately,

SAM. JOHNSON [3]

It took Boswell a month to reply to this, and when he did he wrote from London :

My dear Sir,

I have received your last letter, which, though very short, and by no means complimentary, yet gave me real pleasure, because it contains these words, ' I shall be glad, very glad to see you.'—Surely you have no reason to complain of my publishing a single paragraph [4] of one of

---

[1] *Lewis*, p. 117.
[2] Thus the *Globe* edition of 1914. But the fourth edition reads *now*, which makes better sense.
[3] *Life*, p. 193.          [4] See pp. 112–3.

your letters; the temptation to it was so strong. An
irrevocable grant of your friendship, and your dignifying
my desire of visiting Corsica with the epithet of ' a wise
and noble curiosity ', are to me more valuable than many
of the grants of kings.

But how can you bid me ' empty my head of Corsica '?
My noble-minded friend, do you not feel for an oppressed
nation bravely struggling to be free? Consider fairly
what is the case. The Corsicans never received any
kindness from the Genoese. They never agreed to be
subject to them. They owe them nothing, and when
reduced to an abject state of slavery by force, shall they
not rise in the great cause of liberty, and break the galling
yoke? And shall not every liberal soul be warm for
them? Empty my head of Corsica ! Empty it of honour,
empty it of humanity, empty it of friendship, empty it of
piety. No! while I live, Corsica and the cause of the
brave islanders shall ever employ much of my attention,
shall ever interest me in the sincerest manner. . . .

I am, &c.

James Boswell [1]

And indeed, in the April of 1768, nothing was further
from Boswell's mind than that he should empty his head of
Corsica. In that same month, in addition to a somewhat
mysterious project for sending church-bells to the
islanders,[2] he had approached Lord Hardwicke, of His
Majesty's Opposition, with a view of furthering the cause; [3]
and one month later he was soliciting everyone he knew to
write Essays that should be calculated to keep up the
spirits of the Corsicans.[4] After all, was he not now known
as Corsica Boswell, a figure and a power in the land !

---

[1] *Life*, p. 193.                    [2] *Gentleman's Magazine*, June 1795.
[3] *Letters*, p. 156.                [4] *Ibid.*, p. 157.

C

" I am really the *Great Man* now," he writes to Temple.
. . . " I give admirable dinners and good claret. . . . I
set up my chariot. This is enjoying the fruit of my
labours, and appearing like the friend of Paoli." [1]  In
which character, in addition to preparing the Essays
above referred to (which, under the style of *British Essays
in favour of the Brave Corsicans*, were published late
the following year, and were many of them, I fear, of his
own composition), he was also occupied in more practical
measures, and had, by the August of 1768, succeeded in
raising, by private subscription in Scotland, the quite
extraordinary sum of £700 to provide his protégés with
ordnance.  " The Carron Company has furnished me them
very cheap.  There are two 32 pounders, four 24's, four
18's, and twenty 9 pounders, with 150 ball to each.  It is
really a tollerable train of artillery." [2]

It was; but unfortunately it was already too late.  By a
treaty signed May 15th, 1768, the Genoese had sold their
rights in the island to France, and the French at once took
the necessary steps to secure their bargain.  Paoli wrote to
Boswell that he and his countrymen were prepared to
stand to the last,[2] but Boswell saw immediately that the
only hope for them lay in the intervention of Britain.
He did all he could to bring this about, and in the spring
of the next year departed to Ireland (though his journey
there was a little complicated by his pursuit of her whom
he called *la belle Irlandaise*) to arouse sympathy and to
gather subscriptions.  But though Ireland, as ever, was
much impressed by the spectacle of insurrection, the
British Government would do nothing.  As Lord Holland
remarked, rather tartly : " Foolish as we are, we cannot
be so foolish as to go to war because Mr. Boswell has been
in Corsica." [3]

[1] *Letters*, p. 160.      [2] *Ibid.*, p. 161.      [3] *Tinker*, p. 112.

Soon all was over.  By May 1769 the French had taken
Corte, the capital, and Paoli was a fugitive.  Yet all was
not, perhaps, pure loss, for out of his Irish journey came
Boswell's marriage to his cousin, Margaret Montgomery,
who had accompanied him upon that expedition.

In September, though the game was really played out,
there was one final flourish, and Boswell made his most
celebrated appearance in the Corsican costume, when he
took part in the celebrations at the Shakespeare Jubilee at
Stratford, and was careful to send an account of the whole
thing to the *London Magazine*, which he prefixed with the
very well-known engraving that shows him thus accoutred.
In the same month Paoli arrived in England, and was
received with great acclaim.  The King himself sent for
him, and, among other things, said :  " I have read
Boswell's book, which is well written (*scritto con spirito*).
May I depend upon it as an authentick account ? "
Paoli's reply was both modest and emphatic :  " Your
Majesty may be assured that every thing in that book is
true, except the compliments which Mr. Boswell has been
pleased to pay to his friend." [1]

It is pleasant to be able to add that the British Government treated Paoli handsomely; a pension of £1,200 a
year [2] was granted him, which, according to Horace
Walpole, he owed to Boswell's exertions. [3]  Two years
later, one of Boswell's dreams came true, and the General
paid a visit to Auchinleck.  " You may figure ", wrote
Boswell, " the joy of my worthy father and me at seeing
the Corsican Hero in our romantick groves." [4]  His joy,
no doubt, was unfeigned, but one wishes one could be as
sure of his father's.  According to Walter Scott, old
Auchinleck was accustomed to refer to his heroic guest, in

[1] *Letters*, p. 174.              [2] *Southey*, p. 69.
[3] *Tinker*, p. 112.              [4] *Letters*, p. 184.

unguarded moments, as " a land-louping scoundrel of a Corsican ". [1]

*    *    *    *    *

For the rest of his life, Boswell never quite escaped from the reputation he had acquired by the Corsican adventure. At regular intervals, letters arrived for him from eminent Corsicans who alleged they had seen him on the island, and wished to renew their acquaintance; [2] and his friendship with Paoli waxed ever deeper, so that he had the pleasure on many occasions of being able to observe the juxtaposition, in social intercourse, of his two great exemplars, the Doctor and the General. When his wife died in 1789, the *Gentleman's Magazine* announced the event by describing her as " the wife of the celebrated tourist "; and even so late as the last year of his own life he was being approached by a benevolent inhabitant of the town of Shaftesbury in Dorset, to see whether he could not do something to assist the fortunes of the descendants of the ex-King Theodore who, not very surprisingly, had fallen into indigence. [3]

But before that the affairs of Corsica had taken a new turn. About 1790, Paoli returned to the island, and the British Government, which had for so long turned a deaf ear to Boswell's representations on behalf of his brave islanders, was now keenly interested in the embarrassment that their activities were causing the French. When, in 1793, England at last declared war on the French Republic, this interest became even more practical, and, under Hood, Bastia was besieged, and a large part of the island captured. It was at this point that the event occurred with which we may fittingly close the whole story. Boswell was fifty-four years of age, and had but another year to

[1] *Letters*, p. 184 (footnote).  [2] *Abbott*, pp. 34, 229.  [3] *Ibid.*, p. 159.

live; he was ill, a widower, more deeply plunged than ever in melancholy, and, though the *Life of Johnson* was published, considered himself a hopeless failure. On March 17th, 1794, from his house at No. 47 [1] Great Portland Street, he addressed to Henry Dundas, the Secretary of State, the following proposal : [2]

Dear Sir,

Eleven years are now elapsed since I received from you a letter expressing in very cordial terms your inclination to befriend me in my views of obtaining some promotion . . .

An occasion . . . so peculiar now offers for my applying to you, that I should upbraid myself if I omitted it. The success of His Majesty's forces by sea and land against the French and their adherents in Corsica leaves no doubt that by this time that island is totally free from any subjection to the horrible power to which I am at a loss to give a name. Of course the brave inhabitants will wish to form a connection with Great Britain, which certainly may be of considerable advantage to us. Whatever shall be the nature of that connection, some person must necessarily be appointed there as Minister or Commissioner or under some denomination on the part of this country. Permit me, then, to offer my services, and to request that I may be recommended to His Majesty to be employed in that capacity. My knowledge of Corsica, and my having been the first man by whose means authentick information of its importance was obtained, my long and continued intimacy with General Paoli, and the consideration how agreeable it would be to him and to the people in general, that I should be sent thither, seem, I cannot help thinking, to have such weight as almost to preclude competition;

[1] Now No. 122.                    [2] *Letters*, pp. 459–60.

and should I be so fortunate as to be honoured with a trust which would of all be to me the most pleasing, you may be assured of my utmost attention and zeal to fulfill its duties. . . .

> I am, dear Sir,
>> Your faithful and
>>> most obedient humble servant
>>>> JAMES BOSWELL

But Dundas took no notice, and the office that Boswell sought was given to Sir Gilbert Elliot who, under the style of Commissary Plenipotentiary, received, in the name of King George III, the tender of the Corsican crown.

Thus, though Boswell's characteristic offer was disregarded, he did, at least, have the satisfaction of living to see his beloved Corsica a British dependency. It was not long to remain one. In 1796, just over a year after his death, the British forces evacuated the island. The last Englishman to embark was a commodore named Horatio Nelson.[1] The star of another Corsican was rising, who had in his nonage, in the summer of 1793, first taken up his arms against Paoli. Now his deeds in Italy were on the lips of all men. An age had passed away.

> MORCHARD BISHOP.
>> August, 1950.

[1] *Southey*, p. 107.

# DEDICATION

## TO

# PASCAL PAOLI

## GENERAL OF

# THE CORSICANS

SIR,

DEDICATIONS are for most part the offerings of interested servility, or the effusions of partial zeal; enumerating the virtues of men in whom no virtues can be found, or predicting greatness to those who afterwards pass their days in unambitious indolence, and die leaving no memorial of their existence but a dedication, in which all their merit is confessedly future and which time has turned into a silent reproach.

He who has any experience of mankind, will be cautious to whom he dedicates. Publickly to bestow praise on merit of which the publick is not sensible, or to raise flattering expectations which are never fulfilled, must sink the character of an authour, and make him appear a cringing parasite, or a fond enthusiast.

I am under no apprehensions of that nature, when I inscribe this book to Pascal Paoli. Your virtues, Sir, are universally acknowledged; they dignify the pages

which I venture to present to you; and it is my singular
felicity that my book is the voucher of its dedication.

In thus addressing you, my intention is not to attempt
your panegyrick.   That may in some measure be collected
from my imperfect labours.   But I wish to express to the
world, the admiration and gratitude with which you have
inspired me.

This, Sir, is all the return that I can make for the many
favours which you have deigned to confer upon me.   I
intreat you to receive it as a testimony of my disposition.
I regret that I have neither power nor interest to enable
me to render any essential service to you and to the brave
Corsicans.   I can only assure you of the most fervent
wishes of a private gentleman.   I have the honour to be,
with all respect and affection,

SIR,

Your ever devoted,

obliged humble servant,

JAMES BOSWELL.

Auchinleck,
Ayrshire,
29 October, 1767.

# PREFACE

NO apology shall be made for presenting the world with An Account of Corsica. It has been for some time expected from me; and I own that the ardour of publick curiosity has both encouraged and intimidated me. On my return from visiting Corsica, I found people where-ever I went, desirous to hear what I could tell them concerning that island and its inhabitants. Unwilling to repeat my tale to every company, I thought it best to promise a book which should speak for me.

But I would not take upon me to do this, till I consulted with the General of the nation. I therefore informed him of my design. His answer is perhaps too flattering for me to publish: but I must beg leave to give it as the licence and sanction of this work.

Paoli was pleased to write to me thus; ' Non può esser piu generoso il di lei disegno di pubblicar colle stampe le osservazioni che ha fatte sopra la Corsica. Ella ne ha veduto la fisica situazione, ha potuto esaminare i costumi degli abitanti, e veder dentro le massime del loro governo, di cui conosce la costituzione. Questi popoli con entusiasmo di gratitudine uniranno il loro applauso a quello dell' Europa disingannata. Nothing can be more generous than your design to publish the observations which you have made upon Corsica. You have seen its natural situation, you have been able to study the manners of its inhabitants, and to see intimately the maxims of their government, of which you know the constitution. This people with an enthusiasm of gratitude, will unite their applause with that of undeceived Europe.'

My first intention was to give only a view of the present
state of Corsica, together with Memoirs of its illustrious
General. But by the advice of some learned friends,
whose judgement I respect, I enlarged my plan, and
fixed on that, of the execution of which the publick is now
to judge.

I had before me two French books expressly written on
Corsica. The one ' Histoire de l'Isle de Corse par M. G.
D. C.' printed at Nancy in 1749. The other ' Memoires
Historiques &c. par M. Jaussin Ancien Apoticaire Major; '
printed at Lausanne in 1758. From both of those books I
derived many useful materials. The last of them contains a full and scientifick detail of the natural history
of the island, as also many letters, manifestoes and other
papers : And both of them contain a variety of particulars
with regard to the operations of the French in Corsica. I
had also before me a pretty large collection of remarks,
which I had committed to writing, while I was in the
island.

But I still found my materials deficient in many
respects. I therefore applied to my friends abroad;
and in the mean time directed my studies to such books
as might furnish me with any thing relative to the subject.
I am thus enabled to lay before the world such An Account
of Corsica, as I flatter myself will give some satisfaction;
for, in comparison of the very little that has been hitherto
known concerning that island, this book may be said to
contain a great deal.

It is indeed amazing that an island so considerable,
and in which such noble things have been doing, should
be so imperfectly known. Even the succession of Chiefs
has been unperceived; and because we have read of Paoli
being at the head of the Corsicans many years back, and
Paoli still appears at their head, the command has been

supposed all this time in the person of the same man. Hence all our news-papers have confounded the gallant Pascal Paoli in the vigour of manhood, with the venerable chief his deceased Father Giacinto Paoli. Nay the same errour has found its way into the page of the historian; for Dr. Smollet when mentioning Paoli at the siege of Furiani a few years ago, says he was then past fourscore.

I would in the first place return my most humble thanks to Pascal Paoli, for the various communications with which he has been pleased to favour me; and as I have related his remarkable sayings, I declare upon honour, that I have neither added nor diminished; nay so scrupulous have I been, that I would not make the smallest variation even when my friends thought it would be an improvement. I know with how much pleasure we read what is perfectly authentick.

Count Rivarola was so good as to return me full and distinct answers to a variety of queries which I sent him with regard to many particulars concerning Corsica. I am much indebted to him for this, and particularly so, from the obliging manner in which he did it.

The reverend Mr. Burnaby, chaplain to the British factory at Leghorn, made a tour to Corsica in 1766, at the same time with the honourable and reverend Mr. Hervey now bishop of Cloyne. Mr. Burnaby was absent from Leghorn when I was there, so I had not the pleasure of being personally known to him. But he with great politeness, of his own accord, sent me a copy of the Journal which he made of what he observed in Corsica. I had the satisfaction to find that we agreed in every thing which both of us had considered. But I found in his Journal, observations on several things which I had omitted; and several things which I had remarked, I found set in a clearer light. As Mr. Burnaby was so obliging as to allow me to make what use I pleased of his Journal, I have freely interwoven it into my work.

I acknowledge my obligations to my esteemed friend John Dick Esquire, his Britannick Majesty's Consul at Leghorn, to Signor Gian Quilico Casa Bianca, to the learned Greek physician Signor Stefanopoli, to Colonel Buttafoco, and to the Abbé Rostini. These gentlemen have all contributed their aid in erecting my little monument to liberty.

I am also tq thank an ingenious gentleman who has favoured me with the translations of Seneca's Epigrams. I made application for this favour, in the London Chronicle; and to the honour of literature, I found her votaries very liberal. Several translations were sent, of which I took the liberty to prefer those which had the signature of Patricius, and which were improved by another ingenious correspondent under the signature of Plebeius. By a subsequent application I begged that Patricius would let me know to whom I was obliged for what I considered as a great ornament to my book. He has complied with my request; and I beg leave in this publick manner, to acknowledge that I am indebted for those translations to Thomas Day Esquire, of Berkshire, a gentleman whose situation in life is genteel, and his fortune affluent. I must add that although his verses have not only the fire of youth, but the maturity and correctness of age, Mr. Day is no more than nineteen.

Nor can I omit to express my sense of the candour and politeness with which Sir James Steuart received the remark which I have ventured to make in opposition to a passage concerning the Corsicans, in his Inquiry into the Principles of Political Oeconomy.

I have submitted my book to the revisal of several gentlemen who honour me with their regard, and I am sensible how much it is improved by their corrections. It is therefore my duty to return thanks to the reverend Mr. Wyvill rector of Black Notely in Essex, and to my old and most intimate friend the reverend Mr. Temple rectour of Mamhead in Devonshire. I am also obliged to My Lord Monboddo for many judicious remarks, which his thorough acquaintance with ancient learning enabled him to make. But I am principally indebted to the indulgence and friendly attention of My Lord Hailes, who under the name of Sir David Dalrymple,* has been long known to the world as an able Antiquarian, and an elegant and humourous Essayist; to whom the world has no fault but that he does not give them more of his own writings, when they value them so highly.

I would however have it understood, that although I received the corrections of my friends with deference, I have not always agreed with them. An authour should be glad to hear every candid remark. But I look upon a man as unworthy to write, who has not force of mind to determine for himself. I mention this, that the judgement of the friends I have named may not be considered as connected with every passage in this book.

Writing a book I have found to be like building a house. A man forms a plan, and collects materials. He thinks he has enough to raise a large and stately edifice; but after he has arranged, compacted and polished, his work turns out to be a very small performance. The authour however like the builder, knows how much labour his work has cost him; and therefore estimates it at a much higher rate than other people think it deserves.

I have endeavoured to avoid an ostentatious display

* It is the custom in Scotland to give the Judges of the court of session the title of Lords by the names of their estates. Thus Mr. Burnett is Lord Monboddo, and Sir David Dalrymple is Lord Hailes.

of learning. By the idle and the frivolous indeed, any appearance of learning is called pedantry. But as I do not write for such readers, I pay no regard to their censures. Those by whom I wish to be judged, will, I hope, approve of my adding dignity to Corsica, by shewing its consideration among the ancients, and will not be displeased to find my page sometimes embellished with a seasonable quotation from the Classicks. The translations are ascribed to their proper authours. What are not so ascribed are my own.

It may be necessary to say something in defence of my orthography. Of late it has become the fashion to render our language more neat and trim by leaving out k after c, and u in the last syllable of words which used to end in our. The illustrious Mr. Samuel Johnson, who has alone executed in England what was the task of whole academies in other countries, has been careful in his Dictionary to preserve the k as a mark of Saxon original. He has for most part too, been careful to preserve the u, but he has also omitted it in several words. I have retained the k, and have taken upon me to follow a general rule with regard to words ending in our. Wherever a word originally Latin has been transmitted to us through the medium of the French, I have written it with the characteristical u. An attention to this may appear trivial. But I own I am one of those who are curious in the formation of language in its various modes; and therefore wish that the affinity of English with other tongues may not be forgotten. If this work should at any future period be reprinted, I hope that care will be taken of my orthography.

He who publishes a book, affecting not to be an authour, and professing an indifference for literary fame, may possibly impose upon many people such an idea of his consequence as he wishes may be received. For my part, I should be proud to be known as an authour; and I have an ardent ambition for literary fame; for of all possessions I should imagine literary fame to be the most valuable. A man who has been able to furnish a book which has been approved by the world, has established himself as a respectable character in distant society, without any danger of having that character lessened by the observation of his weaknesses. To preserve an uniform dignity among those who see us every day, is hardly possible; and to aim at it, must put us under the fetters of a perpetual restraint. The authour of an approved book may allow his natural disposition an easy play, and yet indulge the pride of superiour genius when he considers that by those who know him only as an authour, he never ceases to be respected. Such an authour when in his hours of gloom and discontent, may have the consolation to think that his writings are at that very time giving pleasure to numbers; and such an authour may cherish the hope of being remembered after death, which has been a great object to the noblest minds in all ages.

Whether I may merit any portion of literary fame, the publick will judge. Whatever my ambition may be, I trust that my confidence is not too great, nor my hopes too sanguine.

# THE

# JOURNAL

## OF A

# TOUR

## TO

# CORSICA

HAVING resolved to pass some years abroad, for my instruction and entertainment, I conceived a design of visiting the island of Corsica. I wished for something more than just the common course of what is called the tour of Europe; and Corsica occurred to me as a place which no body else had seen, and where I should find what was to be seen no where else, a people actually fighting for liberty, and forming themselves from a poor inconsiderable oppressed nation, into a flourishing and independent state.

When I got into Switzerland, I went to see M. Rousseau. He was then living in romantick retirement, from whence, perhaps, it had been better for him never to have descended. While he was at a distance, his singular eloquence filled our minds with high ideas of the wild philosopher. When he came into the walks of men, we know alas ! how much these ideas suffered.

He entertained me very courteously; for I was recommended to him by my honoured friend the Earl Marischal, with whom I had the happiness of travelling through a part of Germany. I had heard that M. Rousseau had some correspondence with the Corsicans, and had been desired to assist them in forming their laws. I told him my scheme of going to visit them, after I had compleated my tour of Italy; and I insisted that he should give me a letter of introduction. He immediately agreed to do so, whenever I should acquaint him of my time of going thither; for he saw that my enthusiasm for the brave islanders was as warm as his own.

I accordingly wrote to him from Rome, in April 1765, that I had fixed the month of September for my Corsican expedition, and therefore begged of him to send me the letter of introduction, which if he refused, I should certainly go without it, and probably be hanged as a spy. So let him answer for the consequences.

The wild philosopher was a man of his word; and on my arrival at Florence in August, I received the following letter.

A MONSIEUR, MONSIEUR BOSWELL. &c.

A MOTIERS le 30 May, 1765.

'LA crise orageuse ou je me trouve, Monsieur, depuis
' votre depart d'ici, m'a oté le tems de repondre à votre
' premiére lettre, et me laisse à peine celui de repondre en
' peu de mots à la seconde. Pour m'en tenir à ce qui
' presse pour le moment, savoir la recommendation que
' vous desirez en Corse; puisque vous avez le desir de
' visiter ces braves insulaires, vous pourrez vous informer
' à Bastia, de M. Buttafoco capitaine au Regiment Royal
' Italien; il a sa maison à Vescovado, ou il se tient

' assez souvent. C'est un très-galant homme, qui a des
' connoissances et de l'esprit; il suffira de lui montrer
' cette lettre, et je suis sur qu'il vous recevra bien, et
' contribuera à vous faire voir l'isle et ses habitants avec
' satisfaction. Si vous ne trouvez pas M. Buttafoco, et
' que vous vouliez aller tout droit à M. Pascal de Paoli
' general de la nation, vous pouvez egalement lui montrer
' cette lettre, et je suis sur, connoissant la noblesse de son
' caractére, que vous serez très-content de son accueil :
' vous pourrez lui dire même que vous étes aimé de Mylord
' Mareschal d'Ecosse, et que Mylord Mareschal est un
' des plus zelés partizans de la nation Corse. Au reste
' vous n'avez besoin d'autre recommendation près de ces
' Messieurs que votre propre mérite, la nation Corse etant
' naturellement si accueillante et si hospitaliére, que tous
' les etrangers y sont bien venus et caressés.

*    *    *    *    *

' Bons et heureux voyages, sante, gaieté et promt
' retour. Je vous embrasse, Monsieur, de tout mon
' coeur

J. J. ROUSSEAU.

TO MR. BOSWELL &c.

MOTIERS the 30 May, 1765.

' THE stormy crisis in which I have found myself, since
' your departure from this, has not allowed me any
' leisure to answer your first letter, and hardly allows me
' leisure to reply in a few words to your second. To
' confine myself to what is immediately pressing, the
' recommendation which you ask for Corsica; since you
' have a desire to visit those brave islanders, you may

' enquire at Bastia for M. Buttafoco,* captain of the
' Royal Italian Regiment; his house is at Vescovado,
' where he resides pretty often. He is a very worthy
' man, and has both knowledge and genius; it will be
' sufficient to shew him this letter, and I am sure he will
' receive you well, and will contribute to let you see the
' island and its inhabitants with satisfaction. If you
' do not find M. Buttafoco, and will go directly to M.
' Pascal Paoli General of the nation, you may in the same
' manner shew him this letter, and as I know the nobleness
' of his character, I am sure you will be very well pleased
' at your reception. You may even tell him that you are
' liked by My Lord Marischal of Scotland, and that My
' Lord Marischal is one of the most zealous partisans of
' the Corsican nation. You need no other recommenda-
' tion to these gentlemen but your own merit, the Corsicans
' being naturally so courteous and hospitable, that all
' strangers who come among them, are made welcome and
' caressed.

\*       \*       \*       \*       \*

' I wish you agreeable and fortunate travels, health,
' gaiety, and a speedy return. I embrace you Sir with all
' my heart.

JOHN JAMES ROUSSEAU.

* By the time the third edition of Boswell's book came to be
printed, M. Buttafoco had behaved very badly, and so Boswell
caused the following footnote to be added to his text: ' This
man's plausibility imposed upon M. Rousseau and me. But he
has shewn himself to be mean and treacherous; having betrayed
Cascina to the French; for which his memory will ever be in-
famous. They who are possessed of the former editions of this
book, are intreated to erase what I have said of him, first edit.
pages 360 and 361 and second edit. pages 362 and 363.' See also
note on page. 113. [Ed.]

Furnished with these credentials, I was impatient to be with the illustrious Chief. The charms of sweet Siena detained me longer than they should have done. I required the hardy air of Corsica to brace me, after the delights of Tuscany.

I recollect with astonishment how little the real state of Corsica was known, even by those who had good access to know it. An officer of rank in the British navy, who had been in several ports of the island, told me that I run the risque of my life in going among these barbarians; for, that his surgeon's mate went ashore to take the diversion of shooting, and every moment was alarmed by some of the natives, who started from the bushes with loaded guns, and if he had not been protected by Corsican guides, would have certainly blown out his brains.

Nay at Leghorn, which is within a days sailing of Corsica, and has a constant intercourse with it, I found people who dissuaded me from going thither, because it might be dangerous.

I was however under no apprehension in going to Corsica; Count Rivarola the Sardinian consul, who is himself a Corsican, assuring me that the island was then in a very civilized state; and besides, that in the rudest times no Corsican would ever attack a stranger. The Count was so good as to give me most obliging letters to many people in the island. I had now been in several foreign countries. I had found that I was able to accommodate myself to my fellow-creatures of different languages and sentiments. I did not fear that it would be a difficult task for me to make myself easy with the plain and generous Corsicans.

The only danger I saw was, that I might be taken by some of the Barbary Corsairs, and have a tryal of slavery among the Turks at Algiers. I spoke of it to Commodore

Harrison, who commanded the British squadron in the Mediterranean, and was then lying with his ship the Centurion, in the bay of Leghorn. He assured me, that if the Turks did take me, they should not keep me long; but in order to prevent it, he was so good as to grant me a very ample and particular passport; and as it could be of no use if I did not meet the Corsairs, he said very pleasantly when he gave it me, ' I hope, Sir, it will be of no use to you.'

Before I left Leghorn, I could observe, that my tour was looked upon by the Italian politicians in a very serious light, as if truly I had a commission from my Court, to negociate a treaty with the Corsicans. The more I disclaimed any such thing, the more they persevered in affirming it; and I was considered as a very close young man. I therefore allowed them to make a minister of me, till time should undeceive them.

I sailed from Leghorn in a Tuscan vessel, which was going over to Capo Corso for wine. I preferred this to a vessel going to Bastia, because, as I did not know how the French general was affected towards the Corsicans, I was afraid that he might not permit me to go forward to Paoli. I therefore resolved to land on the territories of the nation, and after I had been with the illustrious Chief to pay my respects to the French if I should find it safe.

Though from Leghorn to Corsica, is usually but one day's sailing, there was so dead a calm that it took us two days. The first day was the most tedious. However there were two or three Corsicans aboard, and one of them played on the Citra, which amused me a good deal. At sun-set all the people in the ship sung the Ave Maria, with great devotion and some melody. It was pleasing to enter into the spirit of their religion, and hear them offering up their evening orisons.

The second day we became better acquainted, and more lively and chearful. The worthy Corsicans thought it was proper to give a moral lesson to a young traveller just come from Italy. They told me that in their country I should be treated with the greatest hospitality; but if I attempted to debauch any of their women, I might expect instant death.

I employed myself several hours in rowing, which gave me great spirits. I relished fully my approach to the island, which had acquired an unusual grandeur in my imagination. As long as I can remember any thing, I have heard of ' The malecontents of Corsica, with Paoli at their head.' It was a curious thought that I was just going to see them.

About seven o'clock at night, we landed safely in the harbour of Centuri. I learnt that Signor Giaccomini of this place, to whom I was recommended by Count Rivarola, was just dead. He had made a handsome fortune in the East Indies; and having had a remarkable warmth in the cause of liberty during his whole life, he shewed it in the strongest manner in his last will. He bequeathed a considerable sum of money, and some pieces of ordinance, to the nation. He also left it in charge to his heir, to live in Corsica, and be firm in the patriotick interest; and if ever the island should again be reduced under the power of the Genoese, he ordered him to retire with all his effects to Leghorn. Upon these conditions only could his heir enjoy his estate.

I was directed to the house of Signor Giaccomini's cousin, Signor Antonio Antonetti at Morsiglia, about a mile up the country. The prospect of the mountains covered with vines and olives, was extremely agreeable; and the odour of the myrtle and other aromatick shrubs and flowers that grew all around me, was very refreshing.

As I walked along, I often saw Corsican peasants come suddenly out from the covert; and as they were all armed, I saw how the frightened imagination of the surgeon's mate had raised up so many assassins. Even the man who carried my baggage was armed, and had I been timorous might have alarmed me. But he and I were very good company to each other. As it grew dusky, I repeated to myself these lines from a fine passage in Ariosto.

> E pur per selve oscure e calli obliqui
> Insieme van, senza sospetto aversi.
>
> ARIOST. Canto I.
>
> Together through dark woods and winding ways
> They walk, nor on their hearts suspicion preys.

I delivered Signor Antonetti the letter for his deceased cousin. He read it, and received me with unaffected cordiality, making an apology for my frugal entertainment, but assuring me of a hearty welcome. His true kindly hospitality was also shewn in taking care of my servant, an honest Swiss, who loved to eat and drink well.

I had formed a strange notion that I should see every thing in Corsica totally different from what I had seen in any other country. I was therefore much surprised to find Signor Antonetti's house quite an Italian one, with very good furniture, prints, and copies of some of the famous pictures. In particular, I was struck to find here a small copy from Raphael, of St. Michael and the Dragon. There was no necessity for its being well done. To see the thing at all was what surprised me.

Signor Antonetti gave me an excellent light repast, and a very good bed. He spoke with great strength of the patriotick cause, and with great veneration of the General. I was quite easy, and liked much the opening of my Corsican tour.

The next day, being Sunday, it rained very hard; and I must observe that the Corsicans with all their resolution, are afraid of bad weather, to a degree of effeminacy. I got indeed a droll but just account of this, from one of them. ' Sir, said he, if you were as poor as a ' Corsican, and had but one coat, so as that after being ' wet, you could not put on dry cloaths, you would be ' afraid too.' Signor Antonetti would not allow me to set out while it rained, for, said he, ' Quando si trova ' fuori, patienza; ma di andare fuori è cattivo. If a man ' finds himself abroad, there is no help for it. But to go ' deliberately out, is too much.'

When the day grew a little better, I accompanied Signor Antonetti and his family, to hear mass in the parish church, a very pretty little building, about half a quarter of a mile off.

Signor Antonetti's parish priest was to preach to us, at which I was much pleased, being very curious to hear a Corsican sermon.

Our priest did very well. His text was in the Psalms. ' Descendunt ad infernum viventes. They go down alive ' into the pit.'

After endeavouring to move our passions with a description of the horrours of hell, he told us, ' Saint ' Catherine of Siena wished to be laid on the mouth of this ' dreadful pit, that she might stop it up, so as no more un- ' happy souls should fall into it. I confess, my brethren, ' I have not the zeal of holy Saint Catherine. But I do ' what I can; I warn you how to avoid it.' He then gave us some good practical advice and concluded.

The weather being now cleared up, I took leave of the worthy gentleman to whom I had been a guest. He gave me a letter to Signor Damiano Tomasi Padre del Commune at Pino, the next village. I got a man with an ass to carry my baggage. But such a road I never saw. It was absolutely scrambling along the face of a rock overhanging the sea, upon a path sometimes not above a foot broad. I thought the ass rather retarded me; so I prevailed with the man, to take my portmanteau and other things on his back.

Had I formed my opinion of Corsica from what I saw this morning, I might have been in as bad humour with it, as Seneca was, whose reflections in prose are not inferiour to his epigrams. ' Quid tam nudum inveniri potest, ' quid tam abruptum undique quam hoc saxum? quid ' ad copias respicienti jejunius? quid ad homines imman-' suetius? quid ad ipsum loci situm horridius? Plures ' tamen hîc peregrini quam cives consistunt? usque eò ' ergo commutatio ipsa locorum gravis non est, ut hic ' quoque locus a patria quosdam abduxerit (a). What ' can be found so bare, what so rugged all around as this ' rock? what more barren of provisions? what more rude ' as to its inhabitants? what in the very situation of ' the place more horrible? what in climate more in-' temperate? yet there are more foreigners than natives ' here. So far then is a change of place from being ' disagreeable, that even this place hath brought some ' people away from their country.'

At Pino I was surprised to find myself met by some brisk young fellows drest like English sailors, and speaking English tolerably well. They had been often with cargoes of wine at Leghorn, where they had picked up what they knew of our language, and taken clothes in part of payment for some of their merchandise.

I was cordially entertained at Signor Tomasi's. Throughout all Corsica, except in garrison towns, there is hardly an inn. I met with a single one, about eight

(a) Seneca de Consolatione.

miles from Corte. Before I was accustomed to the Corsican hospitality, I sometimes forgot myself, and imagining I was in a publick house, called for what I wanted, with the tone which one uses in calling to the waiters at a tavern. I did so at Pino, asking for a variety of things at once; when Signora Tomasi perceiving my mistake, looked in my face and smiled, saying with much calmness and good nature, 'Una cosa dopo un altra, Signore. One thing after another, Sir.'

In writing this Journal, I shall not tire my readers, with relating the occurrences of each particular day. It will be much more agreeable to them, to have a free and continued account of what I saw or heard, most worthy of observation.

For some time, I had very curious travelling, mostly on foot, and attended by a couple of stout women, who carried my baggage upon their heads. Every time that I prepared to set out from a village, I could not help laughing, to see the good people eager to have my equipage in order, and roaring out, 'Le Donne, Le Donne. The Women, The Women.'

I had full leisure and the best opportunities to observe every thing, in my progress through the island. I was lodged sometimes in private houses, sometimes in convents, being always well recommended from place to place. The first convent in which I lay, was at Canari. It appeared a little odd at first. But I soon learnt to repair to my dormitory as naturally as if I had been a friar for seven years.

The convents were small decent buildings, suited to the sober ideas of their pious inhabitants. The religious who devoutly endeavour to 'walk with GOD,' are often treated with raillery by those whom pleasure or business prevents from thinking of future and more exalted objects. A little experience of the serenity and peace of mind to be found in convents, would be of use to temper the fire of men of the world.

At Patrimonio I found the seat of a provincial magistracy. The chief judge was there, and entertained me very well. Upon my arrival, the captain of the guard came out, and demanded who I was? I replied 'Inglese. English.' He looked at me seriously, and then said in a tone between regret and upbraiding, 'Inglese, c'erano i 'nostri amici; ma non le sono più. The English; they 'were once our friends; but they are so no more.' I felt for my country, and was abashed before this honest soldier.

At Oletta I visited Count Nicholas Rivarola, brother to my friend at Leghorn. He received me with great kindness, and did every thing in his power to make me easy. I found here a Corsican who thought better of the British, than the captain of the guard at Patrimonio. He talked of our bombarding San Fiorenzo, in favour of the patriots, and willingly gave me his horse for the afternoon, which he said he would not have done to a man of any other nation.

When I came to Morato, I had the pleasure of being made acquainted with Signor Barbaggi, who is married to the niece of Paoli. I found him to be a sensible intelligent well-bred man. The mint of Corsica was in his house. I got specimens of their different kinds of money in silver and copper, and was told that they hoped in a year or two to strike some gold coins. Signor Barbaggi's house was repairing, so I was lodged in the convent. But in the morning returned to breakfast, and had chocolate; and at dinner we had no less than twelve well-drest dishes, served on Dresden china, with a desert, different sorts of wine and a liqueur, all the produce of Corsica.

Signor Barbaggi was frequently repeating to me, that the Corsicans inhabited a rude uncultivated country, and that they lived like Spartans. I begged leave to ask him in what country he could shew me greater luxury than I had seen in his house; and I said I should certainly tell wherever I went, what tables the Corsicans kept, notwithstanding their pretensions to poverty and temperance. A good deal of pleasantry passed upon this. His lady was a genteel woman, and appeared to be agreeable, though very reserved.

From Morato to Corte, I travelled through a wild mountainous rocky country, diversified with some large valleys. I got little beasts for me and my servant, sometimes horses, but oftener mules or asses. We had no bridles, but cords fixed round their necks, with which we managed them as well as we could.

At Corte I waited upon the supreme council, to one of whom, Signor Boccociampe, I had a letter from Signor Barbaggi. I was very politely received, and was conducted to the Franciscan convent, where I got the apartment of Paoli, who was then some days journey beyond the mountains, holding a court of syndicato at a village called Sollacarò.

As the General resided for some time in this convent, the fathers made a better appearance than any I saw in the island. I was principally attended by the Priour, a resolute divine, who had formerly been in the army, and by Padre Giulio, a man of much address, who still favours me with his correspondence.

These fathers have a good vineyard and an excellent garden. They have between 30 and 40 bee-hives in long wooden cases or trunks of trees, with a covering of the bark of the cork tree. When they want honey, they burn a little juniper-wood, the smoak of which makes the bees retire. They then take an iron instrument with a sharp-edged crook at one end of it, and bring out the greatest part of the honey-comb, leaving only a little for the bees, who work the case full again. By taking the honey in this way, they never kill a bee. They seemed much at their ease, living in peace and plenty. I often joked with them with the text which is applied to their order, ' Nihil ' habentes et omnia possidentes. Having nothing, and yet ' possessing all things.'

I went to the choir with them. The service was conducted with propriety, and Padre Giulio played on the organ. On the great altar of their church is a tabernacle carved in wood by a Religious. It is a piece of exquisite workmanship. A Genoese gentleman offered to give them one in silver for it ; but they would not make the exchange.

These fathers have no library worth mentioning; but their convent is large and well built. I looked about with great attention, to see if I could find any inscriptions ; but the only one I found was upon a certain useful edifice.

> Sine necessitate huc non intrate,
> Quia necessaria sumus.

A studied, rhiming, Latin conceit marked upon such a place was truly ludicrous.

I chose to stop a while at Corte, to repose myself after my fatigues, and to see every thing about the capital of Corsica.

The morning after my arrival here, three French deserters desired to speak with me. The foolish fellows had taken it into their heads, that I was come to raise recruits for Scotland, and so they begged to have the honour of going along with me; I suppose with intention to have the honour of running off from me, as they had done from their own regiments.

I received many civilities at Corte from Signor Boccociampe, and from Signor Massesi the Great Chancellor,
whose son Signor Luigi a young gentleman of much
vivacity, and natural politeness, was so good as to attend
me constantly as my conductour. I used to call him my
governour. I liked him much, for as he had never been
out of the island, his ideas were entirely Corsican.

Such of the members of the supreme council as were
in residence during my stay at Corte, I found to be solid
and sagacious, men of penetration and ability, well calculated to assist the General in forming his political plans,
and in turning to the best advantage, the violence and
enterprises of the people.

The university was not then sitting, so I could only see
the rooms, which were shewn me by the Abbé Valentini,
procuratour of the university. The professours were all
absent except one Capuchin father whom I visited at his
convent. It is a tolerable building, with a pretty large
collection of books. There is in the church here a tabernacle carved in wood, in the manner of that at the
Franciscans, but much inferiour to it.

I went up to the castle of Corte. The commandant
very civilly shewed me every part of it. As I wished to see
all things in Corsica, I desired to see even the unhappy
criminals. There were then three in the castle, a man for
the murder of his wife; a married lady who had hired one
of her servants to strangle a woman of whom she was
jealous; and the servant who had actually perpetrated
this barbarous action. They were brought out from their
cells, that I might talk with them. The murderer of
his wife had a stupid hardened appearance, and told me
he did it at the instigation of the devil. The servant
was a poor despicable wretch. He had at first accused his
mistress, but was afterwards prevailed with to deny his

accusation, upon which he was put to the torture, by having lighted matches held between his fingers. This made him return to what he had formerly said, so as to be a strong evidence against his mistress. His hands were so miserably scorched, that he was a piteous object. I asked him why he had committed such a crime, he said, ' Perche era senza spirito. Because I was without understanding.' The lady seemed of a bold and resolute spirit. She spoke to me with great firmness, and denied her guilt, saying with a contemptuous smile, as she pointed to her servant, ' They can force that creature to say what they please.'

The hangman of Corsica was a great curiosity. Being held in the utmost detestation, he durst not live like another inhabitant of the island. He was obliged to take refuge in the castle, and there he was kept in a little corner turret, where he had just room for a miserable bed, and a little bit of fire to dress such victuals for himself as were sufficient to keep him alive, for nobody would have any intercourse with him, but all turned their backs upon him. I went up and looked at him. And a more dirty rueful spectacle I never beheld. He seemed sensible of his situation, and held down his head like an abhorred outcast.

It was a long time before they could get a hangman in Corsica, so that the punishment of the gallows was hardly known, all their criminals being shot. At last this creature whom I saw, who is a Sicilian, came with a message to Paoli. The General who has a wonderful talent for physiognomy, on seeing the man, said immediately to some of the people about him, ' Ecco il boia. Behold our hangman.' He gave orders to ask the man if he would accept of the office, and his answer was, ' My grandfather was a hangman, my father was a hangman.

I have been a hangman myself, and am willing to continue so.' He was therefore immediately put into office, and the ignominious death dispensed by his hands, hath had more effect than twenty executions by fire arms.

It is remarkable that no Corsican would upon any account consent to be hangman. Not the greatest criminals, who might have had their lives upon that condition. Even the wretch, who for a paultry hire, had strangled a woman, would rather submit to death, than do the same action, as the executioner of the law.

When I had seen every thing about Corte, I prepared for my journey over the mountains, that I might be with Paoli. The night before I set out, I recollected that I had forgotten to get a passport, which, in the present situation of Corsica, is still a necessary precaution. After supper therefore the Priour walked with me to Corte, to the house of the Great Chancellor, who ordered the passport to be made out immediately, and while his secretary was writing it, entertained me by reading to me some of the minutes of the general consulta. When the passport was finished, and ready to have the seal put to it, I was much pleased with a beautiful, simple incident. The Chancellor desired a little boy who was playing in the room by us, to run to his mother, and bring the great seal of the kingdom. I thought myself sitting in the house of a Cincinnatus.

Next morning I set out in very good order, having excellent mules, and active clever Corsican guides. The worthy fathers of the convent who treated me in the kindest manner while I was their guest, would also give me some provisions for my journey; so they put up a gourd of their best wine, and some delicious pomegranates. My Corsican guides appeared so hearty, that I often got down

E

and walked along with them, doing just what I saw them
do. When we grew hungry, we threw stones among the
thick branches of the chestnut trees which overshadowed
us, and in that manner we brought down a shower of
chestnuts with which we filled our pockets, and went on
eating them with great relish; and when this made us
thirsty, we lay down by the side of the first brook, put
our mouths to the stream, and drank sufficiently. It
was just being for a little while, one of the ' prisca gens
mortalium, the primitive race of men,' who ran about in
the woods eating acorns and drinking water.

While I stopped to refresh my mules at a little village,
the inhabitants came crouding about me as an ambassadour going to their General. When they were informed
of my country, a strong black fellow among them said,
' Inglese ! sono barbari; non credono in DIO grande.
' English ! they are barbarians; they don't believe in the
' great GOD.' I told him, Excuse me Sir. We do believe
in GOD, and in Jesus Christ too. ' Um, said he, e nel
' Papa? and in the Pope?' No. ' E perche? And
' why?' This was a puzzling question in these circumstances; for there was a great audience to the contro-
versy. I thought I would try a method of my own, and
very gravely replied, ' Perche siamo troppo lontani.
' Because we are too far off.' A very new argument
against the universal infallibility of the Pope. It took
however; for my opponent mused a while, and then said.
' Troppo lontano ! La Sicilia è tanto lontana che l'Inghil-
' terra; e in Sicilia si credono nel Papa. Too far off !
' Why Sicily is as far off as England. Yet in Sicily they
' believe in the Pope.' ' O, said I, noi siamo dieci volte più
' lontani che la Sicilia ! We are ten times farther off than
' Sicily.' ' Aha!' said he; and seemed quite satisfied.
In this manner I got off very well. I question much

whether any of the learned reasonings of our protestant divines would have had so good an effect.

My journey over the mountains was very entertaining. I past some immense ridges and vast woods. I was in great health and spirits, and fully able to enter into the ideas of the brave rude men whom I found in all quarters.

At Bastelica where there is a stately spirited race of people, I had a large company to attend me in the convent. I liked to see their natural frankness and ease; for why should men be afraid of their own species? They came in making an easy bow, placed themselves round the room where I was sitting, rested themselves on their muskets, and immediately entered into conversation with me. They talked very feelingly of the miseries that their country had endured, and complained that they were still but in a state of poverty. I happened at that time to have an unusual flow of spirits; and as one who finds himself amongst utter strangers in a distant country has no timidity, I harangued the men of Bastelica with great fluency. I expatiated on the bravery of the Corsicans, by which they had purchased liberty, the most valuable of all possessions, and rendered themselves glorious over all Europe. Their poverty, I told them, might be remedied by a proper cultivation of their island, and by engaging a little in commerce. But I bid them remember, that they were much happier in their present state than in a state of refinement and vice, and that therefore they should beware of luxury.

What I said had the good fortune to touch them, and several of them repeated the same sentiments much better than I could do. They all expressed their strong attachment to Paoli, and called out in one voice that they were all at his command. I could with pleasure, have passed a long time here.

At Ornano I saw the ruins of the seat where the great Sampiero had his residence. They were a pretty droll society of monks in the convent at Ornano. When I told them that I was an Englishman, ' Aye, aye,' said one of them, 'as was well observed by a reverend bishop, ' when talking of your pretended reformation, Angli olim ' angeli nunc diaboli. The English formerly angels now ' devils.' I looked upon this as an honest effusion of spiritual zeal. The Fathers took good care of me in temporals.

When I at last came within sight of Sollacarò, where Paoli was, I could not help being under considerable anxiety. My ideas of him had been greatly heightened by the conversations I had held with all sorts of people in the island, they having represented him to me as something above humanity. I had the strongest desire to see so exalted a character; but I feared that I should be unable to give a proper account why I had presumed to trouble him with a visit, and that I should sink to nothing before him. I almost wished to go back without seeing him. These workings of sensibility employed my mind till I rode through the village and came up to the house where he was lodged.

Leaving my servant with my guides, I past through the guards, and was met by some of the General's people, who conducted me into an antichamber, where were several gentlemen in waiting. Signor Boccociampe had notified my arrival, and I was shewn into Paoli's room. I found him alone, and was struck with his appearance. He is tall, strong, and well made; of a fair complexion, a sensible, free, and open countenance, and a manly, and noble carriage. He was then in his fortieth year. He was drest in green and gold. He used to wear the common Corsican habit, but on the arrival of the French he thought a little external elegance might be of use to make the government appear in a more respectable light.

He asked me what were my commands for him. I presented him a letter from Count Rivarola, and when he had read it, I shewed him my letter from Rousseau. He was polite, but very reserved. I had stood in the presence of many a prince, but I never had such a trial as in the presence of Paoli. I have already said, that he is a great physiognomist. In consequence of his being in continual danger from treachery and assassination, he has formed a habit of studiously observing every new face. For ten minutes we walked backwards and forwards through the room, hardly saying a word, while he looked at me, with a stedfast, keen and penetrating eye, as if he searched my very soul.

This interview was for a while very severe upon me. I was much relieved when his reserve wore off, and he began to speak more. I then ventured to address him with this compliment to the Corsicans. ' Sir, I am upon ' my travels, and have lately visited Rome. I am come ' from seeing the ruins of one brave and free people : I ' now see the rise of another.'

He received my compliment very graciously; but observed that the Corsicans had no chance of being like the Romans, a great conquering nation, who should extend its empire over half the globe. Their situation, and the modern political systems, rendered this impossible. But, said he, Corsica may be a very happy country.

He expressed a high admiration of M. Rousseau, whom Signor Buttafoco had invited to Corsica, to aid the nation in forming its laws.

It seems M. de Voltaire had reported, in his rallying manner, that the invitation was merely a trick which he had put upon Rousseau. Paoli told me that when he understood this, he himself wrote to Rousseau, enforcing the invitation. Of this affair I shall give a full account in an after part of my Journal.

Some of the nobles who attended him, came into the room, and presently we were told that dinner was served up. The General did me the honour to place me next him. He had a table of fifteen or sixteen covers, having always a good many of the principal men of the island with him. He had an Italian cook who had been long in France; but he chose to have a few plain substantial dishes, avoiding every kind of luxury, and drinking no foreign wine.

I felt myself under some constraint in such a circle of heroes. The General talked a great deal on history and on literature. I soon perceived that he was a fine classical scholar, that his mind was enriched with a variety of knowledge, and that his conversation at meals was instructive and entertaining. Before dinner he conversed in French. He now spoke Italian, in which he is very eloquent.

We retired to another room to drink coffee. My timidity wore off. I no longer anxiously thought of myself; my whole attention was employed in listening to the illustrious commander of a nation.

He recommended me to the care of the Abbé Rostini, who had lived many years in France. Signor Colonna, the lord of the manor here being from home, his house was assigned for me to live in. I was left by myself till near supper time, when I returned to the General, whose conversation improved upon me, as did the society of those about him, with whom I gradually formed an acquaintance.

Every day I felt myself happier. Particular marks of

attention were shewn me as a subject of Great Britain, the report of which went over to Italy, and confirmed the conjectures that I was really an envoy. In the morning I had my chocolate served up upon a silver salver adorned with the arms of Corsica. I dined and supped constantly with the General. I was visited by all the nobility, and whenever I chose to make a little tour, I was attended by a party of guards. I begged of the General not to treat me with so much ceremony; but he insisted upon it.

One day when I rode out I was mounted on Paoli's own horse, with rich furniture of crimson velvet, with broad gold lace, and had my guards marching along with me. I allowed myself to indulge a momentary pride in this parade, as I was curious to experience what could really be the pleasure of state and distinction with which mankind are so strangely intoxicated.

When I returned to the continent after all this greatness, I used to joke with my acquaintance, and tell them that I could not bear to live with them, for they did not treat me with a proper respect.

My time passed here in the most agreeable manner. I enjoyed a sort of luxury of noble sentiment. Paoli became more affable with me. I made myself known to him. I forgot the great distance between us, and had every day some hours of private conversation with him.

From my first setting out on this tour, I wrote down every night what I had observed during the day, throwing together a great deal, that I might afterwards select at leisure.

Of these particulars, the most valuable to my readers, as well as to myself, must surely be the memoirs and remarkable sayings of Paoli, which I am proud to record.

Talking of the Corsican war, ' Sir, said he, if the event

prove happy, we shall be called great defenders of liberty. If the event shall prove unhappy, we shall be called unfortunate rebels.'

The French objected to him that the Corsican nation had no regular troops. We would not have them, said Paoli. We should then have the bravery of this and the other regiment. At present every single man is as a regiment himself. Should the Corsicans be formed into regular troops, we should lose that personal bravery which has produced such actions among us, as in another country would have rendered famous even a Marischal.

I asked him how he could possibly have a soul so superiour to interest. ' It is not superiour, said he; my interest is to gain a name. I know well that he who does good to his country will gain that : and I expect it. Yet could I render this people happy, I would be content to be forgotten. I have an unspeakable pride, " Una superbia indicibile." The approbation of my own heart is enough.'

He said he should have great pleasure in seeing the world, and enjoying the society of the learned, and the accomplished in every country. I asked him how with these dispositions, he could bear to be confined to an island yet in a rude uncivilized state; and instead of participating Attick evenings, ' noctes coenaeque Deûm,' be in a continual course of care and of danger. He replied in one line of Virgil.

Vincet amor patriae laudumque immensa cupido.

This uttered with the fine open Italian pronunciation, and the graceful dignity of his manner, was very noble. I wished to have a statue of him taken at that moment.

I asked him if he understood English. He immediately began and spoke it, which he did tolerably well. When at

Naples, he had known several Irish gentlemen who were officers in that service. Having a great facility in acquiring languages, he learnt English from them. But as he had been now ten years without ever speaking it, he spoke very slow. One could see that he was possessed of the words, but for want of what I may call mechanical practice, he had a difficulty in expressing himself.

I was diverted with his English library. It consisted of
Some broken volumes of the Spectatour and Tatler.
Pope's Essay on Man.
Gulliver's Travels.
A History of France, in old English.
And
Barclay's Apology for the Quakers.
I promised to send him some English books.*

He convinced me how well he understood our language; for I took the liberty to shew him a Memorial which I had drawn up on the advantages to Great Britain from an alliance with Corsica, and he translated this memorial into Italian with the greatest facility. He has since given me more proofs of his knowledge of our tongue by his answers to the letters which I have had the honour to write to him in English, and in particular by a very judicious and ingenious criticism on some of Swift's works.

He was well acquainted with the history of Britain. He had read many of the parliamentary debates, and had even seen a number of the North Briton. He shewed a considerable knowledge of this country, and often intro-

* I have sent him the Works of Harrington, of Sidney, of Addison, of Trenchard, of Gordon, and of other writers in favour of liberty. I have also sent him some of our best books of morality and entertainment, in particular the Works of Mr. Samuel Johnson, with a compleat set of the Spectatour, Tatler and Guardian; and to the University of Corte, I have sent a few of the Greek and Roman Classicks, of the beautiful editions of the Messieurs Foulis at Glasgow.

duced anecdotes and drew comparisons and allusions from Britain.

He said his great object was to form the Corsicans in such a manner that they might have a firm constitution, and might be able to subsist without him. ' Our state, said he, is young, and still requires the leading strings. I am desirous that the Corsicans should be taught to walk of themselves. Therefore when they come to me to ask whom they shall chuse for their Padre del Commune, or other Magistrate, I tell them, You know better than I do, the able and honest men among your neighbours. Consider the consequence of your choice, not only to yourselves in particular, but to the island in general. In this manner I accustom them to feel their own importance as members of the state.'

After representing the severe and melancholy state of oppression under which Corsica had so long groaned, he said, ' We are now to our country like the prophet Elishah stretched over the dead child of the Shunamite, eye to eye, nose to nose, mouth to mouth. It begins to recover warmth, and to revive. I hope it will yet regain full health and vigour.'

I said that things would make a rapid progress, and that we should soon see all the arts and sciences flourish in Corsica. ' Patience Sir, said he. If you saw a man who had fought a hard battle, who was much wounded, who was beaten to the ground, and who with difficulty could lift himself up, it would not be reasonable to ask him to get his hair well drest, and to put on embroidered clothes. Corsica has fought a hard battle, has been much wounded, has been beaten to the ground, and with difficulty can lift herself up. The arts and sciences are like dress and ornament. You cannot expect them from us for some time. But come back twenty or thirty years hence, and we'll shew you arts and sciences, and concerts and assemblies, and fine ladies, and we'll make you fall in love among us, Sir.'

He smiled a good deal, when I told him that I was much surprised to find him so amiable, accomplished, and polite; for although I knew I was to see a great man, I expected to find a rude character, an Attila king of the Goths, or a Luitprand king of the Lombards.

I observed that although he had often a placid smile upon his countenance, he hardly ever laughed. Whether loud laughter in general society be a sign of weakness or rusticity, I cannot say; but I have remarked that real great men, and men of finished behaviour, seldom fall into it.

The variety, and I may say versatility, of the mind of this great man is amazing. One day when I came to pay my respects to him before dinner, I found him in much agitation, with a circle of his nobles around him, and a Corsican standing before him like a criminal before his judge. Paoli immediately turned to me, ' I am glad you are come, Sir. You protestants talk much against our doctrine of transubstantiation. Behold here the miracle of transubstantiation, a Corsican transubstantiated into a Genoese. That unworthy man who now stands before me is a Corsican, who has been long a lieutenant under the Genoese, in Capo Corso. Andrew Doria and all their greatest heroes could not be more violent for the republick than he has been, and all against his country.' Then turning to the man, ' Sir, said he, Corsica makes it a rule to pardon the most unworthy of her children, when they surrender themselves, even when they are forced to do so, as is your case. You have now escaped. But take care. I shall have a strict eye upon you; and if ever you make the least attempt to return to your traiterous practices, you know I can be avenged of you.' He spoke this with the fierceness of a lion, and from the awful darkness of his brow, one could see that his thoughts of vengeance were terrible. Yet when it was over, he all at once resumed his usual appearance, called out, ' andiamo, come along '; went to dinner, and was as chearful and gay as if nothing had happened.

His notions of morality are high and refined, such as become the Father of a nation. Were he a libertine, his influence would soon vanish; for men will never trust the important concerns of society to one they know will do what is hurtful to society for his own pleasures. He told me that his father had brought him up with great strictness, and that he had very seldom deviated from the paths of virtue. That this was not from a defect of feeling and passion, but that his mind being filled with important objects, his passions were employed in more noble pursuits than those of licentious pleasure. I saw from Paoli's example the great art of preserving young men of spirit from the contagion of vice, in which there is often a species of sentiment, ingenuity and enterprise nearly allied to virtuous qualities.

Shew a young man that there is more real spirit in virtue than in vice, and you have a surer hold of him, during his years of impetuosity and passion, than by convincing his judgment of all the rectitude of ethicks.

One day at dinner, he gave us the principal arguments for the being and attributes of GOD. To hear these arguments repeated with graceful energy by the illustrious Paoli in the midst of his heroick nobles, was admirable. I never felt my mind more elevated.

I took occasion to mention the king of Prussia's infidel writings, and in particular his epistle to Marischal Keith. Paoli who often talks with admiration of the greatness of that monarch, instead of uttering any direct censure of what he saw to be wrong in so distinguished a hero, paused a little, and then said with a grave and most expressive look, ' C'est une belle consolation pour un vieux general ' mourant, " En peu de tems vous ne serez plus." It is ' fine consolation for an old general when dying, " In a ' little while you shall be no more." '

He observed that the Epicurean philosophy had produced but one exalted character, whereas Stoicism had been the seminary of great men. What he now said put me in mind of these noble lines of Lucan.

> Hi mores, haec duri immota Catonis
> Secta fuit, servare modum finemque tenere,
> Naturamque sequi, patriaeque impendere vitam,
> Nec sibi sed toti genitum se credere mundo.
> > Lucan. Pharsal. lib. ii. l. 380.

> These were the stricter manners of the man,
> And this the stubborn course in which they ran;
> The golden mean unchanging to pursue,
> Constant to keep the purpos'd end in view;
> Religiously to follow nature's laws,
> And die with pleasure in his country's cause.
> To think he was not for himself design'd,
> But born to be of use to all mankind.
> > Rowe.

When he was asked if he would quit the island of which he had undertaken the protection, supposing a foreign power should create him a Marischal, and make him governour of a province; he replied, ' I hope they will believe I am more honest, or more ambitious; for, said he, to accept of the highest offices under a foreign power would be to serve.'

To have been a colonel, a general or a marischal, said he, ' would have been sufficient for my table, for my taste in dress, for the beauty whom my rank would have entitled me to attend. But it would not have been sufficient for this spirit, for this imagination.' Putting his hand upon his bosom.

He reasoned one day in the midst of his nobles whether the commander of a nation should be married or not. 'If he is married, said he, there is a risqué that he may be distracted by private affairs, and swayed too much by a concern for his family. If he is unmarried, there is a risque that not having the tender attachments of a wife and children, he may sacrifice all to his own ambition.' When I said he ought to marry and have a son to succeed him, 'Sir, said he, what security can I have that my son will think and act as I do? What sort of a son had Cicero, and what had Marcus Aurelius?'

He said to me one day when we were alone, 'I never will marry. I have not the conjugal virtues. Nothing would tempt me to marry, but a woman who should bring me an immense dowry, with which I might assist my country.'

But he spoke much in praise of marriage, as an institution which the experience of ages had found to be the best calculated for the happiness of individuals, and for the good of society. Had he been a private gentleman, he probably would have married, and I am sure would have made as good a husband and father as he does a supreme magistrate and a general. But his arduous and critical situation would not allow him to enjoy domestick felicity. He is wedded to his country, and the Corsicans are his children.

He often talked to me of marriage, told me licentious pleasures were delusive and transient, that I should never be truly happy till I was married, and that he hoped to have a letter from me soon after my return home, acquainting him that I had followed his advice, and was convinced from experience, that he was in the right. With such an engaging condescension did this great man behave to me.

If I could but paint his manner, all my readers would be charmed with him.

He has a mind fitted for philosophical speculations as well as for affairs of state. One evening at supper, he entertained us for some time with some curious reveries and conjectures as to the nature of the intelligence of beasts, with regard to which, he observed human knowledge was as yet very imperfect. He in particular seemed fond of inquiring into the language of the brute creation. He observed that beasts fully communicate their ideas to each other, and that some of them, such as dogs, can form several articulate sounds. In different ages there have been people who pretended to understand the language of birds and beasts. ' Perhaps, said Paoli, in a thousand years we may know this as well as we know things which appeared much more difficult to be known.' I have often since this conversation, indulged myself in such reveries. If it were not liable to ridicule, I would say that an acquaintance with the language of beasts would be a most agreeable acquisition to man, as it would enlarge the circle of his social intercourse.

On my return to Britain I was disappointed to find nothing upon this subject in Doctour Gregory's Comparative View of the State and Faculties of Man with those of the Animal World, which was then just published. My disappointment however was in a good measure made up by a picture of society, drawn by that ingenious and worthy authour, which may be well applied to the Corsicans. ' There is a certain period in the progress of ' society in which mankind appear to the greatest advan- ' tage. In this period, they have the bodily powers, and ' all the animal functions remaining in full vigour. They ' are bold, active, steady, ardent in the love of liberty and ' their native country. Their manners are simple, their

' social affections warm, and though they are greatly
' influenced by the ties of blood, yet they are generous
' and hospitable to strangers. Religion is universally
' regarded among them, though disguised by a variety of
' superstitions (a).'

Paoli was very desirous that I should study the character
of the Corsicans. ' Go among them, said he, the more you
talk with them, you will do me the greater pleasure. Forget the meanness of their apparel. Hear their sentiments.
You will find honour, and sense and abilities among these
poor men.'

His heart grew big when he spoke of his countrymen.
His own great qualities appeared to unusual advantage,
while he described the virtues of those for whose happiness his whole life was employed. ' If, said he, I should
lead into the field an army of Corsicans against an army
double their number, let me speak a few words to the
Corsicans, to remind them of the honour of their country
and of their brave forefathers, I do not say that they would
conquer, but I am sure that not a man of them would give
way. The Corsicans, said he, have a steady resolution
that would amaze you. I wish you could see one of them
die. It is a proverb among the Genoese, " I Corsi meritano
la furca e la sanno soffrire. The Corsicans deserve the
gallows, and they fear not to meet it." There is a real
compliment to us in this saying.'

He told me, that in Corsica, criminals are put to death
four and twenty hours after sentence is pronounced against
them. This, said he, may not be over catholick, but it is
humane.

He went on, and gave me several instances of the
Corsican spirit.

A sergeant, said he, who fell in one of our desperate
(a) Preface to Comparative View, p. 8.

actions, when just a dying, wrote to me thus. ' I salute
you. Take care of my aged father. In two hours I
shall be with the rest who have bravely died for their
country.'

A Corsican gentleman who had been taken prisoner
by the Genoese, was thrown into a dark dungeon, where he
was chained to the ground. While he was in this dismal
situation, the Genoese sent a message to him, that if he
would accept of a commission in their service, he might
have it. ' No, said he. Were I to accept of your offer, it
' would be with a determined purpose to take the first
' opportunity of returning to the service of my country.
' But I will not accept of it. For I would not have my
' countrymen even suspect that I could be one moment
' unfaithful.' And he remained in his dungeon. Paoli
went on. ' I defy Rome, Sparta or Thebes to shew me
thirty years of such patriotism as Corsica can boast.
Though the affection between relations is exceedingly
strong in the Corsicans, they will give up their nearest
relations for the good of their country, and sacrifice such as
have deserted to the Genoese.'

He gave me a noble instance of a Corsican's feeling
and greatness of mind. ' A criminal, said he, was con-
demned to die. His nephew came to me with a lady of
distinction, that she might solicit his pardon. The
nephew's anxiety made him think that the lady did not
speak with sufficient force and earnestness. He therefore
advanced, and addressed himself to me, " Sir, is it proper
for me to speak? " as if he felt that it was unlawful to
make such an application. I bid him go on. " Sir, said
he, with the deepest concern, may I beg the life of my
uncle? If it is granted, his relations will make a
gift to the state of a thousand zechins. We will furnish
fifty soldiers in pay during the siege of Furiani. We will

F

agree that my uncle shall be banished, and will engage that he shall never return to the island." I knew the nephew to be a man of worth, and I answered him: You are acquainted with the circumstances of this case. Such is my confidence in you, that if you will say that giving your uncle a pardon would be just, useful or honourable for Corsica, I promise you it shall be granted. He turned about, burst into tears, and left me, saying, " Non vorrei vendere l'onore della patria per mille zechini. I would not have the honour of our country sold for a thousand zechins." And his uncle suffered.'

Although the General was one of the constituent members of the court of syndicato, he seldom took his chair. He remained in his own apartment; and if any of those whose suits were determined by the syndicato were not pleased with the sentence, they had an audience of Paoli, who never failed to convince them that justice had been done them. This appeared to me a necessary indulgence in the infancy of government. The Corsicans having been so long in a state of anarchy, could not all at once submit their minds to the regular authority of justice. They would submit implicitly to Paoli, because they love and venerate him. But such a submission is in reality being governed by their passions. They submit to one for whom they have a personal regard. They cannot be said to be perfectly civilized till they submit to the determinations of their magistrates as officers of the state, entrusted with the administration of justice. By convincing them that the magistrates judge with abilities and uprightness, Paoli accustoms the Corsicans to have that salutary confidence in their rulers, which is necessary for securing respect and stability to the government.

After having said much in praise of the Corsicans, ' Come, said he, you shall have a proof of what I tell you.

There is a crowd in the next room, waiting for admittance to me. I will call in the first I see, and you shall hear him.' He who chanced to present himself, was a venerable old man. The General shook him by the hand, and bid him good day, with an easy kindness that gave the aged peasant full encouragement to talk to his Excellency with freedom. Paoli bid him not mind me, but say on. The old man then told him that there had been an unlucky tumult in the village where he lived, and that two of his sons were killed. That looking upon this as a heavy misfortune, but without malice on the part of those who deprived him of his sons, he was willing to have allowed it to pass without inquiry. But his wife anxious for revenge, had made an application to have them apprehended and punished. That he gave his Excellency this trouble to intreat that the greatest care might be taken, lest in the heat of enmity among his neighbours, any body should be punished as guilty of the blood of his sons, who was really innocent of it. There was something so generous in this sentiment, while at the same time the old man seemed full of grief for the loss of his children, that it touched my heart in the most sensible manner. Paoli looked at me with complacency and a kind of amiable triumph on the behaviour of the old man, who had a flow of words and a vivacity of gesture which fully justified what Petrus Cyrnaeus hath said of the Corsican eloquence ; ' Diceres omnes esse bonos causidicos. You would say ' they are all good pleaders.'

I found Paoli had reason to wish that I should talk much with his countrymen, as it gave me a higher opinion both of him and of them. Thuanus has justly said, ' Sunt ' mobilia Corsorum ingenia. The dispositions of the ' Corsicans are changeable.' Yet after ten years, their attachment to Paoli is as strong as at the first. Nay, they

have an enthusiastick admiration of him. 'Questo
'grand' uomo mandato per DIO a liberare la patria. This
'great man whom GOD hath sent to free our country,'
was the manner in which they expressed themselves to me
concerning him.

Those who attended on Paoli were all men of sense and
abilities in their different departments. Some of them
had been in foreign service. One of them, Signor Suzzoni,
had been long in Germany. He spoke German to me, and
recalled to my mind, the happy days which I have past
among that plain, honest, brave people, who of all nations
in the world, receive strangers with the greatest cordiality.
Signor Gian Quilico Casa Bianca, of the most ancient
Corsican nobility, was much my friend. He instructed
me fully with regard to the Corsican government.
He had even the patience to sit by me while I wrote
down an account of it, which from conversations with
Paoli, I afterwards enlarged and improved. I received
many civilities from the Abbé Rostini, a man of literature,
and distinguished no less for the excellency of his heart.
His saying of Paoli deserves to be remembered. 'Nous
'ne craignons pas que notre General nous trompe ni
'qu'il se laisse tromper. We are not afraid that our
'General will deceive us, nor that he will let himself be
'deceived.'

I also received civilities from Father Guelfucci of the
order of Servites, a man whose talents and virtues, united
with a singular decency and sweetness of manners, have
raised him to the honourable station of secretary to the
General. Indeed all the gentlemen here behaved to me
in the most obliging manner. We walked, rode, and went
a shooting together.

The peasants and soldiers were all frank, open, lively
and bold, with a certain roughness of manner which

agrees well with their character, and is far from being displeasing. The General gave me an admirable instance of their plain and natural, solid good sense. A young French Marquis, very rich and very vain, came over to Corsica. He had a sovereign contempt for the barbarous inhabitants, and strutted about (andava a passo misurato) with prodigious airs of consequence. The Corsicans beheld him with a smile of ridicule, and said, ' Let him alone, he is young.'

The Corsican peasants and soldiers are very fond of baiting cattle with the large mountain dogs. This keeps up a ferocity among them which totally extinguishes fear. I have seen a Corsican in the very heat of a baiting, run in, drive off the dogs, seize the half-frantick animal by the horns, and lead it away. The common people did not seem much given to diversions. I observed some of them in the great hall of the house of Colonna where I was lodged, amusing themselves with playing at a sort of draughts in a very curious manner. They drew upon the floor with chalk, a sufficient number of squares, chalking one all over, and leaving one open, alternately; and instead of black men and white, they had bits of stone and bits of wood. It was an admirable burlesque on gaming.

The chief satisfaction of these islanders when not engaged in war or in hunting, seemed to be that of lying at their ease in the open air, recounting tales of the bravery of their countrymen, and singing songs in honour of the Corsicans, and against the Genoese. Even in the night they will continue this pastime in the open air, unless rain forces them to retire into their houses.

The ambasciadore Inglese, The English ambassadour, as the good peasants and soldiers used to call me, became a great favourite among them. I got a Corsican dress made, in which I walked about with an air of true satisfaction.

The General did me the honour to present me with his own pistols, made in the island, all of Corsican wood and iron, and of excellent workmanship. I had every other accoutrement. I even got one of the shells which had often sounded the alarm to liberty. I preserve them all with great care.

The Corsican peasants and soldiers were quite free and easy with me. Numbers of them used to come and see me of a morning, and just go out and in as they pleased. I did every thing in my power to make them fond of the British, and bid them hope for an alliance with us. They asked me a thousand questions about my country, all which I chearfully answered as well as I could.

One day they would needs hear me play upon my German flute. To have told my honest natural visitants, Really gentlemen I play very ill, and put on such airs as we do in our genteel companies, would have been highly ridiculous. I therefore immediately complied with their request. I gave them one or two Italian airs, and then some of our beautiful old Scots tunes, Gilderoy, the Lass of Patie's Mill, Corn riggs are Bonny. The pathetick simplicity and pastoral gaiety of the Scots musick, will always please those who have the genuine feelings of nature. The Corsicans were charmed with the specimens I gave them, though I may now say that they were very indifferently performed.

My good friends insisted also to have an English song from me. I endeavoured to please them in this too, and was very lucky in that which occurred to me. I sung them ' Hearts of oak are our ships, Hearts of oak are our men.' I translated it into Italian for them, and never did I see men so delighted with a song as the Corsicans were with Hearts of oak. ' Cuore di quercia, cried they, ' bravo Inglese.' It was quite a joyous riot. I fancied

myself to be a recruiting sea-officer. I fancied all my
chorus of Corsicans aboard the British fleet.

Paoli talked very highly on preserving the independency
of Corsica. ' We may, said he, have foreign powers for
our friends; but they must be " Amici fuori di casa.
Friends at arm's length." We may make an alliance,
but we will not submit ourselves to the dominion of the
greatest nation in Europe. This people who have done so
much for liberty, would be hewn in pieces man by man,
rather than allow Corsica to be sunk into the territories of
another country. Some years ago, when a false rumour
was spread that I had a design to yield up Corsica to the
Emperour, a Corsican came to me, and addressed me in
great agitation. " What ! shall the blood of so many
heroes, who have sacrificed their lives for the freedom of
Corsica, serve only to tinge the purple of a foreign
prince ! " '

I mentioned to him the scheme of an alliance between
Great Britain and Corsica. Paoli with politeness and
dignity waved the subject, by saying, ' The less assistance
we have from allies, the greater our glory.' He seemed
hurt by our treatment of his country. He mentioned the
severe proclamation at the last peace, in which the brave
islanders were called the Rebels of Corsica. He said with
a conscious pride and proper feeling, ' Rebels ! I did not
expect that from Great Britain.'

He however showed his great respect for the British
nation, and I could see he wished much to be in friendship
with us. When I asked him what I could possibly do
in return for all his goodness to me, he replied, ' Sola-
mente disingannate il suo corte. Only undeceive your
court. Tell them what you have seen here. They will
be curious to ask you. A man come from Corsica will
be like a man come from the Antipodes.'

I expressed such hopes as a man of sensibility would in my situation naturally form. He saw at least one Briton devoted to his cause. I threw out many flattering ideas of future political events, imaged the British and the Corsicans strictly united both in commerce and in war, and described the blunt kindness and admiration with which the hearty, generous common people of England would treat the brave Corsicans.

I insensibly got the better of his reserve upon this head. My flow of gay ideas relaxed his severity, and brightened up his humour. ' Do you remember, said he, the little people in Asia who were in danger of being oppressed by the great king of Assyria, till they addressed themselves to the Romans. And the Romans, with the noble spirit of a great and free nation, stood forth, and would not suffer the great king to destroy the little people, but made an alliance with them? '

He made no observations upon this beautiful piece of history. It was easy to see his allusion to his own nation and ours.

When the General related this piece of history to me, I was negligent enough not to ask him what little people he meant. As the story made a strong impression upon me, upon my return to Britain I searched a variety of books to try if I could find it, but in vain. I therefore took the liberty in one of my letters to Paoli, to beg he would let me know it. He told me the little people was the Jews, that the story was related by several ancient authours, but that I would find it told with most precision and energy in the eighth chapter of the first book of the Maccabees.

The first book of the Maccabees, though not received into the Protestant canon, is allowed by all the learned to be an authentick history. I have read Paoli's favourite

story with much satisfaction, and, as in several circumstances, it very well applies to Great Britain and Corsica,
is told with great eloquence, and furnishes a fine model
for an alliance, I shall make no apology for transcribing
the most interesting verses.

‘ Now Judas had heard of the fame of the Romans,
‘ that they were mighty and valiant men, and such as
‘ would lovingly accept all that joined themselves unto
‘ them, and make a league of amity with all that came unto
‘ them.

‘ And that they were men of great valour. It was
‘ told him also of their wars and noble acts which they
‘ had done amongst the Galatians, and how they had
‘ conquered them, and brought them under tribute.

‘ And what they had done in the country of Spain,
‘ for the winning of the mines of the silver and gold which
‘ are there.

‘ And that by their policy and patience they had
‘ conquered all the place, though it were very far from them.

‘ It was told him besides, how they destroyed and
‘ brought under their dominion, all other kingdoms and
‘ isles that at any time resisted them.

‘ But with their friends, and such as relied upon them,
‘ they kept amity : and that they had conquered king-
‘ doms both far and near, insomuch as all that heard of
‘ their name were afraid of them :

‘ Also, that whom they would help to a kingdom, those
‘ reign ; and whom again they would, they displace :
‘ finally, that they were greatly exalted :

‘ Moreover, how they had made for themselves a senate-
‘ house, wherein three hundred and twenty men sat in
‘ council dayly, consulting alway for the people, to the
‘ end that they might be well ordered.

‘ In consideration of these things Judas chose Eupole-

' mus the son of John, the son of Accos, and Jason the son
' of Eleazar, and sent them to Rome, to make a league of
' amity and confederacy with them,

' And to intreat them that they would take the yoke
' from them, for they saw that the kingdom of the Grecians
' did oppress Israel with servitude.

' They went therefore to Rome, which was a very great
' journey, and came into the senate, where they spake, and
' said,

' Judas Maccabeus, with his brethren, and the people
' of the Jews, have sent us unto you, to make a con-
' federacy and peace with you, and that we might be
' registered your confederates and friends.

' So that matter pleased the Romans well.

' And this is the copy of the epistle which the senate
' wrote back again, in tables of brass, and sent to Jeru-
' salem, that there they might have by them a memorial
' of peace and confederacy.

' Good success be to the Romans, and to the people of
' the Jews, by sea and by land for ever. The sword also,
' and enemy be far from them.

' If there come first any war upon the Romans, or any
' of their confederates, throughout all their dominions,

' The people of the Jews shall help them, as the time
' shall be appointed, with all their heart.

' Neither shall they give any thing unto them that
' make war upon them, or aid them with victuals, weapons,
' money or ships, as it hath seemed good unto the Romans,
' but they shall keep their covenant, without taking any
' thing therefore.

' In the same manner also, if war come first upon the
' nation of the Jews, the Romans shall help them with all
' their heart, according as the time shall be appointed
' them.

' Neither shall victuals be given to them that take
' part against them, or weapons, or money, or ships, as it
' hath seemed good to the Romans; but they shall keep
' their covenants, and that without deceit.

' According to these articles did the Romans make a
' covenant with the people of the Jews.

' Howbeit, if hereafter the one party or the other, shall
' think meet to add or diminish any thing they may do it
' at their pleasures, and whatsoever they shall add or take
' away, shall be ratified.

' And, as touching the evils that Demetrius doth to the
' Jews, we have written unto him, saying, Wherefore hast
' thou made thy yoke heavy upon our friends and con-
' federates, the Jews?

' If therefore they complain any more against thee, we
' will do them justice, and fight with thee by sea and by
' land.'

I will venture to ask whether the Romans appear, in
any one instance of their history, more truly great than
they do here.

Paoli said, ' If a man would preserve the generous glow
of patriotism, he must not reason too much. Mareschal
Saxe reasoned; and carried the arms of France into the
heart of Germany, his own country. I act from sentiment, not from reasonings.'

' Virtuous sentiments and habits, said he, are beyond
philosophical reasonings, which are not so strong, and are
continually varying. If all the professours in Europe
were formed into one society, it would no doubt be a
society very respectable, and we should there be entertained with the best moral lessons. Yet I believe I
should find more real virtue in a society of good peasants
in some little village in the heart of your island. It might be
said of these two societies, as was said of Demosthenes and

Themistocles, ' Illius dicta, hujus facta magis valebant.
' The one was powerful in words, but the other in deeds.'

This kind of conversation led me to tell him how much
I had suffered from anxious speculations. With a mind
naturally inclined to melancholy, and a keen desire of
inquiry, I had intensely applied myself to metaphysical
researches, and reasoned beyond my depth, on such
subjects as it is not given to man to know. I told him I
had rendered my mind a camera obscura, that in the very
heat of youth I felt the ' non est tanti ', the ' omnia vanitas '
of one who has exhausted all the sweets of his being, and
is weary with dull repetition. I told him that I had almost
become for ever incapable of taking a part in active life.

' All this, said Paoli, is melancholy. I have also studied
metaphysicks. I know the arguments for fate and free-
will, for the materiality and immateriality of the soul, and
even the subtile arguments for and against the existence
of matter. Ma lasciamo queste dispute ai oziosi. But
let us leave these disputes to the idle. Io tengo sempre
fermo un gran pensiero. I hold always firm one great
object. I never feel a moment of despondency.'

The contemplation of such a character really existing,
was of more service to me than all I had been able to
draw from books, from conversation, or from the exertions
of my own mind. I had often formed the idea of a man
continually such, as I could conceive in my best moments.
But this idea appeared like the ideas we are taught in the
schools to form of things which may exist, but do not ;
of seas of milk, and ships of amber. But I saw my highest
idea realized in Paoli. It was impossible for me, speculate
as I pleased, to have a little opinion of human nature in
him.

One morning I remember, I came in upon him without
ceremony, while he was dressing. I was glad to have an

opportunity of seeing him in those teasing moments, when according to the Duke de Rochefoucault, no man is a hero to his valet de chambre.  That lively nobleman who has a malicious pleasure in endeavouring to divest human nature of its dignity, by exhibiting partial views, and exaggerating faults, would have owned that Paoli was every moment of his life a hero.

Paoli told me that from his earliest years, he had in view the important station which he now holds; so that his sentiments must ever have been great.  I asked him how one of such elevated thoughts could submit with any degree of patience, to the unmeaning ceremonies and poor discourse of genteel society, which he certainly was obliged to do while an officer at Naples.  ' O, said he, I managed it very easily.  Ero connosciuto per una testa singolare, I was known to be a singular man.  I talked and joked, and was merry; but I never sat down to play; I went and came as I pleased.  The mirth I like is what is easy and unaffected.  Je ne puis souffrir long temps les diseurs de bons mots.  I cannot endure long the sayers of good things.'

How much superiour is this great man's idea of agreeable conversation to that of professed wits, who are continually straining for smart remarks, and lively repartees.  They put themselves to much pain in order to please, and yet please less than if they would just appear as they naturally feel themselves.  A company of professed wits has always appeared to me, like a company of artificers employed in some very nice and difficult work, which they are under a necessity of performing.

Though calm and fully master of himself, Paoli is animated with an extraordinary degree of vivacity. Except when indisposed or greatly fatigued, he never sits down but at meals.  He is perpetually in motion, walking briskly backwards and forwards. Mr. Samuel Johnson, whose comprehensive and vigorous understanding, has by long observation, attained to a perfect knowledge of human nature, when treating of biography, has this reflection. ' There are many invisible circumstances ' which, whether we read as enquiries after natural or ' moral knowledge; whether we intend to enlarge our ' science, or increase our virtue, are more important than ' publick occurrences. Thus Sallust, the great master of ' nature, has not forgotten in his account of Catiline, ' to remark, that " his walk was now quick, and again ' slow," as an indication of a mind revolving something ' with violent commotion (a).' Ever mindful of the wisdom of the Rambler, I have accustomed myself to mark the small peculiarities of character. Paoli's being perpetually in motion, nay his being so agitated that, as the same Sallust also says of Catiline, ' Neque vigiliis, ' neque quietibus sedari poterat. He could not be ' quieted either by watching or by repose,' are indications of his being as active and indefatigable as Catiline, but from a very different cause. The conspiratour from schemes of ruin and destruction to Rome; the patriot from schemes of liberty and felicity to Corsica.

Paoli told me that the vivacity of his mind was such, that he could not study above ten minutes at a time. ' La testa mi rompa. My head is like to break,' said he. ' I can never write my lively ideas with my own hand. In writing, they escape from my mind. I call the Abbé Guelfucci, Allons presto, pigliate li pensieri. Come quickly, take my thoughts; and he writes them.'

Paoli has a memory like that of Themistocles; for I was assured that he knows the names of almost all the people in the island, their characters, and their connec-

(a) Rambler, Number 60.

tions. His memory as a man of learning, is no less un-common. He has the best part of the classicks by heart, and he has a happy talent in applying them with propriety, which is rarely to be found. This talent is not always to be reckoned pedantry. The instances in which Paoli is shewn to display it, are a proof to the contrary.

I have heard Paoli recount the revolutions of one of the ancient states, with an energy and a rapidity which shewed him to be master of the subject, to be perfectly acquainted with every spring and movement of the various events. I have heard him give what the French call ' Une catalogue raisonnée ' of the most distinguished men in antiquity. His characters of them were concise, nervous and just. I regret that the fire with which he spoke upon such occasions, so dazzled me that I could not recollect his sayings so as to write them down when I retired from his presence.

He just lives in the times of antiquity. He said to me, ' A young man who would form his mind to glory, must not read modern memoirs; mà Plutarcho, mà Tito Livio; but Plutarch and Titus Livius.'

I have seen him fall into a sort of reverie, and break out into sallies of the grandest and noblest enthusiasm. I recollect two instances of this. ' What a thought? that thousands owe their happiness to you ! ' And throwing himself into an attitude, as if he saw the lofty mountain of fame before him. ' THERE, is my object; (pointing to the summit) if I fall, I fall at least THERE (pointing a good way up) magnis tamen excidit ausis.'

I ventured to reason like a libertine, that I might be confirmed in virtuous principles by so illustrious a pre-ceptour. I made light of moral feelings. I argued that conscience was vague and uncertain; that there was hardly any vice but what men might be found who have been guilty of it without remorse. ' But, said he, there is no man who has not a horrour at some vice. Different vices and different virtues have the strongest impression, on different men; Ma il virtù in astratto è il nutrimento dei nostri cuori. But virtue in the abstract, is the food of our hearts.'

Talking of Providence, he said to me with that earnestness with which a man speaks who is anxious to be believed, ' I tell you on the word of an honest man, it is impossible for me not to be persuaded that GOD interposes to give freedom to Corsica. A people oppressed like the Corsicans, are certainly worthy of divine assistance. When we were in the most desperate circumstances, I never lost courage, trusting as I did in Providence.' I ventured to object; But why has not Providence interposed sooner? He replied with a noble, serious, and devout air, ' Because his ways are unsearchable. I adore him for what he hath done. I revere him in what he hath not done.'

I gave Paoli the character of my revered friend Mr. Samuel Johnson. I have often regretted that illustrious men, such as humanity produces a few times in the revolution of many ages, should not see each other; and when such arise in the same age, though at the distance of half the globe, I have been astonished how they could forbear to meet.

' As steel sharpeneth steel, so doth a man the coun-
' tenance of his friend,' says the wise monarch. What an idea may we not form of an interview between such a scholar and philosopher as Mr. Johnson, and such a legislatour and general as Paoli !

I repeated to Paoli several of Mr. Johnson's sayings, so remarkable for strong sense and original humour. I now recollect these two.

When I told Mr. Johnson that a certain authour affected in conversation to maintain, that there was no distinction between virtue and vice, he said, ' Why Sir, if the fellow ' does not think as he speaks, he is lying; and I see not ' what honour he can propose to himself from having the ' character of a lyar. But if he does really think that ' there is no distinction between virtue and vice, why Sir, ' when he leaves our houses let us count our spoons.'

Of modern infidels and innovatours, he said, ' Sir, ' these are all vain men, and will gratify themselves at any ' expence. Truth will not afford sufficient food to their ' vanity; so they have betaken themselves to errour. ' Truth, Sir, is a cow which will yield such people no more ' milk, and so they are gone to milk the bull.'

I felt an elation of mind to see Paoli delighted with the sayings of Mr. Johnson, and to hear him translate them with Italian energy to the Corsican heroes.

I repeated Mr. Johnson's sayings as nearly as I could, in his own peculiar forcible language, for which, prejudiced or little criticks have taken upon them to find fault with him. He is above making any answer to them, but I have found a sufficient answer in a general remark in one of his excellent papers. ' Difference of thoughts ' will produce difference of language. He that thinks with ' more extent than another, will want words of larger ' meaning '(a).

I hope to be pardoned for this digression, wherein I pay a just tribute of veneration and gratitude to one from whose writings and conversation I have received instructions of which I experience the value in every scene of my life.

During Paoli's administration, there have been few laws made in Corsica. He mentioned one which he has

(a) Idler, number 70.

G

found very efficacious in curbing that vindictive spirit of the Corsicans, of which I have said a good deal in a former part of this work. There was among the Corsicans a most dreadful species of revenge, called ' Vendetta trasversa, Collateral revenge,' which Petrus Cyrnaeus candidly acknowledges. It was this. If a man had received an injury, and could not find a proper opportunity to be revenged on his enemy personally, he revenged himself on one of his enemy's relations. So barbarous a practice, was the source of innumerable assassinations. Paoli knowing that the point of honour was every thing to the Corsicans, opposed it to the progress of the blackest of crimes, fortified by long habits. He made a law, by which it was provided, that this collateral revenge should not only be punished with death, as ordinary murther, but the memory of the offender should be disgraced for ever by a pillar of infamy. He also had it enacted that the same statute should extend to the violatours of an oath of reconciliation, once made.

By thus combating a vice so destructive, he has, by a kind of shock of opposite passions, reduced the fiery Corsicans to a state of mildness, and he assured me that they were now all fully sensible of the equity of that law.

While I was at Sollacarò, information was received, that the poor wretch who strangled the woman at the instigation of his mistress, had consented to accept of his life, upon condition of becoming hangman. This made a great noise among the Corsicans, who were enraged at the creature, and said their nation was now disgraced. Paoli did not think so. He said to me ' I am glad of this. It will be of service. It will contribute to form us to a just subordination. We have as yet too great an equality among us. As we must have Corsican taylours and

Corsican shoemakers, we must also have a Corsican hangman.'

I could not help being of a different opinion. The occupations of a taylour and a shoemaker, though mean, are not odious. When I afterwards met M. Rousseau in England, and made him a report of my Corsican expedition, he agreed with me in thinking that it would be something noble for the brave islanders, to be able to say that there was not a Corsican but who would rather suffer death, than become a hangman; and he also agreed with me, that it might have a good effect to have always a Genoese for the hangman of Corsica.

I must however do the Genoese the justice to observe, that Paoli told me, that even one of them had suffered death in Corsica, rather than consent to become hangman. When I, from a keenness natural enough in a Briton born with an abhorrence at tyranny, talked with violence against the Genoese, Paoli said with a moderation and candour which ought to do him honour even with the republick, ' It is true the Genoese are our enemies; but let us not forget, that they are the descendants of those worthies, who carried their arms beyond the Hellespont.'

There is one circumstance in Paoli's character which I present to my readers with caution, knowing how much it may be ridiculed, in an age when mankind are so fond of incredulity, that they seem to pique themselves in contracting their circle of belief as much as possible. But I consider this infidel rage as but a temporary mode of the human understanding, and am well persuaded that e'er long we shall return to a more calm philosophy.

I own I cannot help thinking that though we may boast some improvements in science, and in short, superiour degrees of knowledge in things where our faculties can fully reach, yet we should not assume to ourselves sounder judgements than those of our fathers; I will therefore venture to relate that Paoli has at times extraordinary impressions of distant and future events.

The way in which I discovered it, was this. Being very desirous of studying so exalted a character, I so far presumed upon his goodness to me, as to take the liberty of asking him a thousand questions with regard to the most minute and private circumstances of his life. Having asked him one day when some of his nobles were present, whether a mind so active as his was not employed even in sleep, and if he used to dream much, Signor Casa Bianca said with an air and tone which implied something of importance, ' Sì, si sogna. Yes, he dreams.' And upon my asking him to explain his meaning, he told me that the General had often seen in his dreams, what afterwards came to pass. Paoli confirmed this by several instances. Said he, ' I can give you no clear explanation of it. I only tell you facts. Sometimes I have been mistaken, but in general, these visions have proved true. I cannot say what may be the agency of invisible spirits. They certainly must know more than we do; and there is nothing absurd in supposing that GOD should permit them to communicate their knowledge to us.'

He went into a most curious and pleasing disquisition on a subject, which the late ingenious Mr. Baxter has treated in a very philosophical manner, in his Inquiry into the Nature of the Human Soul; a book which may be read with as much delight, and surely with more advantage than the works of those who endeavour to destroy our belief. Belief is favourable to the human mind, were it for nothing else but to furnish it entertainment. An infidel I should think, must frequently suffer from ennui.

It was perhaps affectation in Socrates to say, that all he had learned to know was that he knew nothing. But surely it is a mark of wisdom, to be sensible of the limited extent of human knowledge, to examine with reverence the ways of GOD, nor presumptuously reject any opinion which has been held by the judicious and the learned, because it has been made a cloak for artifice, or had a variety of fictions raised upon it, by credulity.

Old Feltham says, ' Every dream is not to be counted ' of; nor yet are all to be cast away with contempt. I ' would neither be a stoick, superstitious in all; nor yet an ' epicure, considerate of none (a).' And after observing how much the ancients attended to the interpretation of dreams, he adds, ' Were it not for the power of the gospel, ' in crying down the vains (b) of men, it would appear a ' wonder how a science so pleasing to humanity, should fall ' so quite to ruin (c).'

The mysterious circumstance in Paoli's character which I have ventured to relate, is universally believed in Corsica. The inhabitants of that island, like the Italians, express themselves much by signs. When I asked one of them, if there had been many instances of the General's fore-seeing future events, he grasped a large bunch of his hair, and replied, ' Tante, Signore, So many Sir.'

It may be said that the General has industriously pro-pagated this opinion, in order that he might have more authority in civilizing a rude and ferocious people; as Lycurgus pretended to have the sanction of the oracle of Delphos; as Numa gave it out that he had frequent interviews with the nymph Egeria; or as Marius per-suaded the Romans, that he received divine communica-

(a) Feltham's Resolves, Cent. I. Resol. 52.
(b) He means vanity.
(c) Feltham's Resolves, Cent. I. Resol. 52.

tions from a hind.   But I cannot allow myself to suppose that Paoli ever required the aid of pious frauds.

Paoli though never familiar, has the most perfect ease of behaviour.   This is a mark of a real great character. The distance and reserve which some of our modern nobility affect, is, because nobility is now little else than a name in comparison of what it was in ancient times.   In ancient times, noblemen lived at their country seats, like princes, in hospitable grandeur.   They were men of power, and every one of them could bring hundreds of followers into the field.   They were then open and affable.   Some of our modern nobility are so anxious to preserve an appearance of dignity which they are sensible cannot bear an examination, that they are afraid to let you come near them.   Paoli is not so.   Those about him come into his apartment at all hours, wake him, help him on with his clothes, are perfectly free from restraint; yet they know their distance, and awed by his real greatness, never lose their respect for him.

Though thus easy of access, particular care is taken against such attempts upon the life of the illustrious Chief, as he has good reason to apprehend from the Genoese, who have so often employed assassination merely in a political view, and who would gain so much by assassinating Paoli. A certain number of soldiers are continually on guard upon him; and as still closer guards, he has some faithful Corsican dogs.   Of these five or six sleep, some in his chamber, and some at the outside of the chamber-door. He treats them with great kindness, and they are strongly attached to him.   They are extremely sagacious, and know all his friends and attendants.   Were any person to approach the General during the darkness of the night, they would instantly tear him in pieces.

Having dogs for his attendants, is another circumstance about Paoli similar to the heroes of antiquity. Homer represents Telemachus so attended.

> δύω κύνες ἀργοὶ ἔποντο.
>
> HOMER. Odyss. lib. ii. l. 11.
>
> Two dogs a faithful guard attend behind.
>
> POPE.

But the description given of the family of Patroclus applies better to Paoli.

> Ἐννέα τῷ γε ἄνακτι τραπεζῆες κύνες ἦσαν.
>
> HOMER. Iliad lib. xxiii. l. 173.
>
> nine large dogs domestick at his board.
>
> POPE.

Mr. Pope in his notes on the second book of the Odyssey, is much pleased with dogs being introduced, as it furnishes an agreeable instance of ancient simplicity. He observes that Virgil thought this circumstance worthy of his imitation, in describing old Evander. So we read of Syphax, general of the Numidians, ' Syphax inter duos ' canes stans, Scipionem appellavit (a). Syphax standing ' between two dogs called to Scipio.'

Talking of courage, he made a very just distinction between constitutional courage and courage from reflection. ' Sir Thomas More, said he, would not probably have mounted a breach so well as a sergeant who had never thought of death. But a sergeant would not on a scaffold, have shewn the calm resolution of Sir Thomas More.'

On this subject he told me a very remarkable anecdote, which happened during the last war in Italy. At the siege of Tortona, the commander of the army which lay

(a) I mention this on the authority of an excellent scholar, and one of our best writers, Mr. Joseph Warton in his notes on the Aeneid; for I have not been able to find the passage in Livy which he quotes.

before the town, ordered Carew an Irish officer in the service of Naples, to advance with a detachment to a particular post. Having given his orders, he whispered to Carew, ' Sir, I know you to be a gallant man. I have ' therefore put you upon this duty. I tell you in con- ' fidence, it is certain death for you all. I place you there ' to make the enemy spring a mine below you.' Carew made a bow to the general, and led on his men in silence to the dreadful post. He there stood with an undaunted countenance, and having called to one of the soldiers for a draught of wine, ' Here, said he, I drink to all those who bravely fall in battle.' Fortunately at that instant Tortona capitulated, and Carew escaped. But he had thus a full opportunity of displaying a rare instance of determined intrepidity. It is with pleasure that I record an anecdote so much to the honour of a gentleman of that nation, on which illiberal reflections are too often thrown, by those of whom it little deserves them. Whatever may be the rough jokes of wealthy insolence, or the envious sarcasms of needy jealousy, the Irish have ever been, and will continue to be, highly regarded upon the continent.

Paoli's personal authority among the Corsicans struck me much. I have seen a croud of them with eagerness and impetuosity, endeavouring to approach him, as if they would have burst into his apartment by force. In vain did the guards attempt to restrain them; but when he called to them in a tone of firmness, ' Non c'è ora ricorso, No audience now,' they were hushed at once.

He one afternoon gave us an entertaining dissertation on the ancient art of war. He observed that the ancients allowed of little baggage, which they very properly called ' impedimenta '; whereas the moderns burthen themselves with it to such a degree, that 50,000 of our present soldiers are allowed as much baggage as was formerly thought sufficient for all the armies of the Roman empire. He said it was good for soldiers to be heavy armed, as it renders them proportionably robust; and he remarked that when the Romans lightened their arms, the troops became enfeebled. He made a very curious observation with regard to the towers full of armed men, which we are told were borne on the backs of their elephants. He said it must be a mistake; for if the towers were broad, there would not be room for them on the backs of elephants; for he and a friend who was an able calculatour, had measured a very large elephant at Naples, and made a computation of the space necessary to hold the number of men said to be contained in those towers, and they found that the back of the broadest elephant would not be sufficient, after making the fullest allowance for what might be hung by ballance on either side of the animal. If again the towers were high, they would fall; for he did not think it at all probable, that the Romans had the art of tying on such monstrous machines at a time when they had not learnt the use even of girths to their saddles. He said he did not give too much credit to the figures on Trajan's pillar, many of which were undoubtedly false. He said it was his opinion, that those towers were only drawn by the elephants; an opinion founded in probability, and free from the difficulties of that which has been commonly received.

Talking of various schemes of life, fit for a man of spirit and education; I mentioned to him that of being a foreign minister. He said he thought it a very agreeable employment for a man of parts and address, during some years of his life. ' In that situation, said he, a man will insensibly attain to a greater knowledge of men and manners, and a more perfect acquaintance with the politicks of Europe.

He will be promoted according to the returns which he makes to his court. They must be accurate, distinct, without fire or ornament. He may subjoin his own opinion, but he must do it with great modesty. The ministry at home are proud.'

He said the greatest happiness was not in glory, but in goodness; and that Penn in his American colony, where he had established a people in quiet and contentment, was happier than Alexander the Great after destroying multitudes at the conquest of Thebes. He observed that the history of Alexander is obscure and dubious; for his captains who divided his kingdom, were too busy to record his life and actions, and would at any rate wish to render him odious to posterity.

Never was I so thoroughly sensible of my own defects as while I was in Corsica. I felt how small were my abilities, and how little I knew. Ambitious to be the companion of Paoli, and to understand a country and a people which roused me so much, I wished to be a Sir James MacDonald (a).

The last day which I spent with Paoli, appeared of inestimable value. I thought him more than usually great and amiable, when I was upon the eve of parting from him. The night before my departure, a little incident happened which shewed him in a most agreeable light. When the servants were bringing in the desert after supper, one of them chanced to let fall a plate of walnuts. Instead of flying into a passion at what the man could not help,

(a) Sir James MacDonald baronet of the isle of Sky, who at the age of one and twenty, had the learning and abilities of a Professour and a statesman, with the accomplishments of a man of the world. Eton and Oxford will ever remember him as one of their greatest ornaments. He was well known to the most distinguished in Europe, but was carried off from all their expectations. He died at Frescati, near Rome, in 1765. Had he lived a little longer, I believe I should have prevailed with him to visit Corsica.

Paoli said with a smile, ' No matter '; and turning to me, ' It is a good sign for you, Sir, Tempus est spargere nuces, It is time to scatter walnuts. It is a matrimonial omen : You must go home to your own country, and marry some fine woman whom you really like. I shall rejoice to hear of it.'

This was a pretty allusion to the Roman ceremony at weddings, of scattering walnuts. So Virgil's Damon says,

Mopse novas incide faces : tibi ducitur uxor.
Sparge marite nuces : tibi deserit Hesperus Oetam.
VIRG. Eclog. viii. l. 30.

Thy bride comes forth ! begin the festal rites !
The walnuts strew ! prepare the nuptial lights !
O envied husband, now thy bliss is nigh !
Behold for thee bright Hesper mounts the sky !
WARTON.

When I again asked Paoli if it was possible for me in any way to shew him my great respect and attachment, he replied, ' Ricordatevi che Io vi sia amico, e scrivetemi. Remember that I am your friend, and write to me.' I said I hoped that when he honoured me with a letter, he would write not only as a commander, but as a philosopher and a man of letters. He took me by the hand, and said, ' As a friend.' I dare not transcribe from my private notes the feelings which I had at this interview. I should perhaps appear too enthusiastick. I took leave of Paoli with regret and agitation, not without some hopes of seeing him again. From having known intimately so exalted a character, my sentiments of human nature were raised, while, by a sort of contagion, I felt an honest ardour to distinguish myself, and be useful, as far as my situation and abilities would allow; and I was, for the rest of my life, set free from a slavish timidity in the presence of great men, for where shall I find a man greater than Paoli?

When I set out from Sollacarò, I felt myself a good deal indisposed. The old house of Colonna, like the family of its master, was much decayed; so that both wind and rain found their way into my bed-chamber. From this I contracted a severe cold, which ended in a tertian ague. There was no help for it. I might well submit to some inconveniences, where I had enjoyed so much happiness.

I was accompanied a part of the road by a great swarthy priest, who had never been out of Corsica. He was a very Hercules for strength and resolution. He and two other Corsicans took a castle garrisoned by no less than fifteen Genoese. Indeed the Corsicans have such a contempt for their enemies, that I have heard them say, ' Basterebbero le donne contra i Genovesi, Our women would be enough against the Genoese.' This priest was a bluff, hearty, roaring fellow, troubled neither with knowledge nor care. He was ever and anon shewing me how stoutly his nag could caper. He always rode some paces before me, and sat in an attitude half turned round, with his hand clapped upon the crupper. Then he would burst out with comical songs about the devil and the Genoese, and I don't know what all. In short, notwithstanding my feverishness, he kept me laughing whether I would or no.

I was returning to Corte, but I varied my road a little from the way I had come, going more upon the low country, and nearer the western shore.

At Cauro I had a fine view of Ajaccio and its environs. My ague was some time of forming, so I had frequent intervals of ease, which I employed in observing whatever occurred. I was lodged at Cauro in the house of Signor Peraldi of Ajaccio, who received me with great politeness.

I found here another provincial magistracy. Before supper, Signor Peraldi and a young Abbé of Ajaccio entertained me with some airs on the violin. After they had shewn me their taste in fine improved musick, they gave me some original Corsican airs, and at my desire, they brought up four of the guards of the magistracy, and made them shew me a Corsican dance. It was truly savage. They thumped with their heels, sprung upon their toes, brandished their arms, wheeled and leaped with the most violent gesticulations. It gave me the idea of an admirable war dance.

During this journey I had very bad weather. I cannot forget the worthy rectour of Cuttoli, whose house afforded me a hospitable retreat, when wet to the skin, and quite overcome by the severity of the storm, which my sickness made me little able to resist. He was directly such a venerable hermit as we read of in the old romances. His figure and manner interested me at first sight. I found he was a man well respected in the island, and that the General did him the honour to correspond with him. He gave me a simple collation of eggs, chestnuts and wine, and was very liberal of his ham and other more substantial victuals to my servant. The honest Swiss was by this time very well pleased to have his face turned towards the continent. He was heartily tired of seeing foreign parts, and meeting with scanty meals and hard beds, in an island which he could not comprehend the pleasure of visiting. He said to me, ' Si J'etois encore une fois retourné à mon pais parmi ces montagnes de Suisse dont monsieur fait tant des plaisanteries, Je verrai qui m'en-gagera à les quitter. If I were once more at home in my own country, among those mountains of Switzerland, on which you have had so many jokes, I will see who shall prevail with me to quit them.'

The General out of his great politeness, would not allow me to travel without a couple of chosen guards to attend me in case of any accidents. I made them my companions, to relieve the tediousness of my journey. One of them called Ambrosio, was a strange iron-coloured fearless creature. He had been much in war; careless of wounds, he was cooly intent on destroying the enemy. He told me, as a good anecdote, that having been so lucky as to get a view of two Genoese exactly in a line, he took his aim, and shot them both through the head at once. He talked of this, just as one would talk of shooting a couple of crows. I was sure I needed be under no apprehension; but I don't know how, I desired Ambrosio to march before me that I might see him.

I was upon my guard how I treated him. But as sickness frets one's temper, I sometimes forgot myself, and called him ' bestia, blockhead '; and once when he was at a loss which way to go, at a wild woody part of the country, I fell into a passion, and called to him, ' Mi maraviglio che un uomo si bravo può esser si stupido. I am amazed that so brave a man can be so stupid.' However by afterwards calling him friend, and speaking softly. to him, I soon made him forget my ill humour, and we proceeded as before.

Paoli had also been so good as to make me a present of one of his dogs, a strong and fierce animal. But he was too old to take an attachment to me, and I lost him between Lyons and Paris. The General has promised me a young one, to be a guard at Auchinleck.

At Bogognano I came upon the same road I had formerly travelled from Corte, where I arrived safe after all my fatigues. My good fathers of the Franciscan convent, received me like an old acquaintance, and shewed a kind concern at my illness. I sent my respects to the great

Chancellor, who returned me a note, of which I insert a translation as a specimen of the hearty civility to be found among the highest in Corsica.

'Many congratulations to Mr. Boswell on his return from beyond the mountains, from his servant Massesi, who is at the same time very sorry for his indisposition, which he is persuaded has been occasioned by his severe journey. He however flatters himself, that when Mr. Boswell has reposed himself a little, he will recover his usual health. In the mean time he has taken the liberty to send him a couple of fowls, which he hopes he will honour with his acceptance, as he will need some refreshment this evening. He wishes him a good night, as does his little servant Luiggi, who will attend him to-morrow, to discharge his duty.'

My ague distressed me so much, that I was confined to the convent for several days. I did not however weary. I was visited by the Great Chancellor, and several others of the civil magistrates, and by Padre Mariani rectour of the university, a man of learning and abilities, as a proof of which, he had been three years at Madrid in the character of secretary to the General of the Franciscans. I remember a very eloquent expression of his, on the state of his country, ' Corsica, said he, has for many years past, been bleeding at all her veins. They are now closed. But after being so severely exhausted, it will take some time before she can recover perfect strength.' I was also visited by Padre Leonardo, of whose animating discourse I have made mention in a former part of this book.

Indeed I should not have been at a loss though my very reverend fathers had been all my society. I was not in the least looked upon as a heretick. Difference of faith was forgotten in hospitality. I went about the convent as if I had been in my own house; and the fathers, without any impropriety of mirth, were yet as chearful as I could desire.

I had two surgeons to attend me at Corte, a Corsican and a Piedmontese; and I got a little Jesuit's bark from the spiceria or apothecary's shop, of the Capuchin convent. I did not however expect to be effectually cured, till I should get to Bastia. I found it was perfectly safe for me to go thither. There was a kind of truce between the Corsicans and the French. Paoli had held two amicable conferences with M. de Marboeuf their commander in chief, and was so well with him, that he gave me a letter of recommendation to him.

On one of the days that my ague disturbed me least, I walked from the convent to Corte, purposely to write a letter to Mr. Samuel Johnson. I told my revered friend, that from a kind of superstition agreeable in a certain degree to him, as well as to myself, I had during my travels, written to him from LOCA SOLENNIA, places in some measure sacred. That as I had written to him from the Tomb of Melancthon, sacred to learning and piety, I now wrote to him from the palace of Pascal Paoli, sacred to wisdom and liberty; knowing that however his political principles may have been represented, he had always a generous zeal for the common rights of humanity. I gave him a sketch of the great things I had seen in Corsica, and promised him a more ample relation.

Mr. Johnson was pleased with what I wrote here; for I received at Paris an answer from him which I keep as a valuable charter. ' When you return, you will return to ' an unaltered, and I hope, unalterable friend. All that ' you have to fear from me, is the vexation of disappointing ' me. No man loves to frustrate expectations which ' have been formed in his favour, and the pleasure which I ' promise myself from your journals and remarks, is

' so great, that perhaps no degree of attention or discern-
' ment will be sufficient to afford it.   Come home however
' and take your chance.   I long to see you, and to hear
' you; and hope that we shall not be so long separated
' again.   Come home, and expect such a welcome as is
' due to him whom a wise and noble curiosity has led
' where perhaps, no native of this country ever was
' before.'

I at length set out for Bastia.   I went the first night
to Rostino, hoping to have found there Signor Clemente de'
Paoli.   But unluckily he had gone upon a visit to his
daughter; so that I had not an opportunity of seeing this
extraordinary personage, of whom I have given so full an
account, for a great part of which I am indebted to Mr.
Burnaby.

Next day I reached Vescovato, where I was received
by Signor Buttafoco,* who proved superiour to the
character I had conceived of him from the letter of M.
Rousseau.   I found in him the incorrupted virtues of the
brave islander, with the improvements of the continent.
I found him, in short, to be a man of principle, abilities
and knowledge; and at the same time a man of the world.
He is now deservedly raised to the rank of colonel of the
Royal Corsicans, in the service of France.

I past some days with Signor Buttafoco, from whose
conversation I received so much pleasure, that I in a great
measure forgot my ague.

As various discourses have been held in Europe, con-

* As explained in the note on page 52, Boswell had revised his
opinion of Signor Buttafoco by the time the third edition of his
book was preparing, and so this passage, in that edition, omits
everything that follows the asterisk above, down to the words
' forgot my ague ', and substitutes, instead : ' colonel of the Royal
Corsicans in the service of France, with whom I past some days.'
[Ed.]

H

cerning an invitation given to M. Rousseau to come to
Corsica; and as that affair was conducted by Signor
Buttafoco, who shewed me the whole correspondence
between him and M. Rousseau, I am enabled to give a
distinct account of it.

M. Rousseau in his Political Treatise, entitled Du
CONTRACT SOCIAL, has the following observation. ' Il est
encore en Europe un pays capable de législation; c'est
l'isle de Corse.  La valeur et la constance avec laquelle
ce brave peuple a su recouvrer et défendre sa liberté
mériteroit bien que quelque homme sage lui apprit à la
conserver.  J'ai quelque pressentiment qu'un jour cette
petite isle etonnera l'Europe (a).  There is yet one
country in Europe, capable of legislation; and that is the
island of Corsica.  The valour and the constancy with
which that brave people hath recovered and defended its
liberty, would well deserve that some wise man should
teach them how to preserve it.   I have some presentiment
that one day that little island will astonish Europe.'

Signor Buttafoco, upon this, wrote to M. Rousseau,
returning him thanks for the honour he had done to the
Corsican nation, and strongly inviting him to come over,
and be that wise man who should illuminate their minds.

I was allowed to take a copy of the wild philosopher's
answer to this invitation; it is written with his usual
eloquence.

' Il est superflu, Monsieur, de chercher à exciter mon
' zele pour l'entreprise que vous me proposez.  Sa seule
' idée m'eleve l'ame et me transporte.  Je croirois la
' reste de mes jours bien noblement, bien vertueusement
' et bien heureusement employés.  Je croirois meme
' avoir bien racheté l'inutilité des autres, si je pouvois
' rendre ce triste reste bon en quelque chose à vos braves

(a) Du Contract Social. liv. ii. chap. 10.

' compàtriotes; si je pouvois concourir par quelque
' conseil utile aux vûes de votre digne Chef et aux votres;
' de ce coté là donc soyez sur de moi. Ma vie et mon
' coeur sont à vous.'

   ' It is superfluous, Sir, to endeavour to excite my zeal
' for the undertaking which you propose to me. The
' very idea of it elevates my soul and transports me. I
' should esteem the rest of my days very nobly, very
' virtuously, and very happily employed. I should even
' think that I well redeemed the inutility of many of my
' days that are past, if I could render these sad remains of
' any advantage to your brave countrymen. If by any
' useful advice, I could concur in the views of your
' worthy Chief, and in yours, so far then you may be
' sure of me. My life and my heart are devoted to you.'

   Such were the first effusions of Rousseau. Yet before
he concluded even this first letter, he made a great many
complaints of his adversities and persecutions, and started
a variety of difficulties as to the proposed enterprise.

   The correspondence was kept up for some time, but the
enthusiasm of the paradoxical philosopher gradually
subsiding, the scheme came to nothing.

   As I have formerly observed, M. de Voltaire thought
proper to exercise his pleasantry upon occasion of this
proposal, in order to vex the grave Rousseau, whom he
never could bear. I remember he used to talk of him with
a satyrical smile, and call him, ' Ce Garçon, That Lad'; I
find this among my notes of M. de Voltaire's conversations,
when I was with him at his Chateau de Ferney, where he
entertains with the elegance rather of a real prince than
of a poetical one.

   To have Voltaire's assertion contradicted by a letter
under Paoli's own hand, was no doubt a sufficient satisfaction to Rousseau.

From the account which I have attempted to give of the present constitution of Corsica, and of its illustrious Legislatour and General, it may well be conceived that the scheme of bringing M. Rousseau into that island, was magnified to an extravagant degree by the reports of the continent. It was said, that Rousseau was to be made no less than a Solon by the Corsicans, who were implicitly to receive from him a code of laws.

This was by no means the scheme. Paoli was too able a man to submit the legislation of his country to one who was an entire stranger to the people, the manners, and in short to every thing in the island. Nay I know well that Paoli pays more regard to what has been tried by the experience of ages, than to the most beautiful ideal systems. Besides, the Corsicans were not all at once to be moulded at will. They were to be gradually prepared, and by one law laying the foundation for another, a compleat fabrick of jurisprudence was to be formed.

Paoli's intention was to grant a generous asylum to Rousseau, to avail himself of the shining talents which appeared in his writings, by consulting with him, and catching the lights of his rich imagination, from many of which he might derive improvements to those plans which his own wisdom had laid down.

But what he had principally in view, was to employ the pen of Rousseau in recording the heroick actions of the brave islanders. It is to be regretted that this project did not take place. The father of the present colonel Buttafoco made large collections for many years back. These are carefully preserved, and when joined to those made by the Abbé Rostini, would furnish ample materials for a History of Corsica. This, adorned with the genius of Rousseau, would have been one of the noblest monuments of modern times.

Signor Buttafoco accompanied me to Bastia. It was comfortable to enter a good warm town after my fatigues. We went to the house of Signor Morelli, a counsellor at law here, with whom we supped. I was lodged for that night by a friend of Signor Buttafoco, in another part of the town.

Next morning I waited on M. de Marboeuf. Signor Buttafoco introduced me to him, and I presented him the letter of recommendation from Paoli. He gave me a most polite reception. The brilliancy of his levee pleased me; it was a scene so different from those which I had been for some time accustomed to see. It was like passing at once from a rude and early age, to a polished modern age; from the mountains of Corsica, to the banks of the Seine.

My ague was now become so violent, that it got the better of me altogether. I was obliged to ask the French general's permission to have a chair set for me in the circle. When M. de Marboeuf was informed of my being ill, he had the goodness to ask me to stay in his house till I should recover; 'I insist upon it, said he; I have a warm room for you. My servants will get you bouillons, and every thing proper for a sick man; and we have an excellent physician.' I mention all these circumstances to shew the goodness of M. de Marboeuf, to whom I shall ever consider myself as under great obligations. His invitation was given in so kind and cordial a manner, that I willingly accepted of it.

I found M. de Marboeuf a worthy open-hearted Frenchman. It is a common and a very just remark, that one of the most agreeable characters in the world is a Frenchman who has served long in the army, and has arrived at that age when the fire of youth is properly tempered. Such a character is gay without levity, and judicious without severity. Such a character was the Count de Marboeuf, of an ancient family in Britanny, where there is more plainness of character than among the other French. He had been Gentilhomme de la Chambre to the worthy King Stanislaus.

He took charge of me as if he had been my near relation. He furnished me with books and every thing he could think of to amuse me. While the physician ordered me to be kept very quiet, M. de Marboeuf would allow nobody to go near me, but payed me a friendly visit alone. As I grew better, he gradually increased my society, bringing with him more and more of his officers; so that I had at last the honour of very large companies in my apartment. The officers were polite agreeable men : some of them had been prisoners in England, during the last war. One of them was a Chevalier de St. Louis, of the name of Douglas, a descendant of the illustrious house of Douglas in Scotland, by a branch settled near to Lyons. This gentleman often came and sat with me. The idea of our being in some sort countrymen, was pleasing to us both.

I found here an English woman of Penrith in Cumberland. When the Highlanders marched through that country in the year 1745, she had married a soldier of the French picquets in the very midst of all the confusion and danger, and when she could hardly understand one word he said. Such freaks will love sometimes take.

> Sic visum Veneri; cui placet impares
> Formas atque animos sub juga aënea
> Saevo mittere cum joco.
>
> HORAT. lib. I. Od. 33.

> So Venus wills, whose power controuls
> The fond affections of our souls;
> With sportive cruelty she binds
> Unequal forms, unequal minds.
>
> FRANCIS.

M. de la Chapelle was the physician who attended me. He had been several years physician to the army at Minorca, and had now the same office in Corsica. I called him the physician of the isles. He was indeed an excellent one. That gayeté de coeur which the French enjoy, runs through all their professions. I remember the phrase of an English common soldier who told me, ' that at the battle of Fontenoy, his captain received a shot in the breast, and fell, said the soldier, with his spontoon in his hand, as prettily killed as ever I see'd a gentleman.' The soldier's phrase might be used in talking of almost every thing which the French do. I may say I was prettily cured by M. de la Chapelle.

But I think myself bound to relate a circumstance which shews him and his nation in the genteelest light. Though he attended me with the greatest assiduity, yet, when I was going away, he would not accept of a single Louis d'or. ' No Sir, said he, I am nobly paid by my king. I am physician to his army here. If I can at the same time, be of service to the people of the country, or to any gentleman who may come among us, I am happy. But I must be excused from taking money.' M. Brion the surgeon major behaved in the same manner.

As soon as I had gathered a little strength, I walked about as well as I could; and saw what was to be seen at Bastia. Signor Morelli was remarkably obliging. He made me presents of books and antiques, and of every other curiosity relating to Corsica. I never saw a more generous man. Signor Caraffa, a Corsican officer in the service of France, with the order of St. Louis, was also very obliging. Having made a longer stay in Corsica than I intended, my finances were exhausted, and he let me have as much money as I pleased. M. Barlé, secretary to M. de Marboeuf, was also very obliging. In short, I know not how to express my thankfulness to all the good people whom I saw at Bastia.

The French seemed to agree very well with the Corsicans. Of old, those islanders were much indebted to the interposition of France, in their favour. But since the days of Sampiero, there have been many variances between them. A singular one happened in the reign of Lewis XIV. The Pope's Corsican guards in some fit of passion insulted the French ambassadour at Rome. The superb monarch resolved to revenge this outrage. But Pope Alexander VII. foreseeing the consequences, agreed to the conditions required by France; which were, that the Corsican guards should be obliged to depart the ecclesiastical state, that the nation should be declared incapable ever to serve the holy see, and, that opposite to their ancient guard-house, should be erected a pyramid inscribed with their disgrace (a).

Le Brun, whose royal genius could magnify and enrich every circumstance in honour of his sovereign, has given this story as a medaillon on one of the compartments of the great gallery at Versailles. France appears with a stately air, shewing to Rome the design of the pyramid; and Rome, though bearing a shield marked S. P. Q. R. receives the design with most submissive humility.

I wish that France had never done the Corsicans greater harm than depriving them of the honour of being the pope's guards. Boisseux and Maillebois cannot easily be forgotten; nor can the brave islanders be blamed for complaining that a powerful nation should interpose to retard their obtaining entire possession of their country, and of undisturbed freedom.

M. de Marboeuf appeared to conduct himself with the greatest prudence and moderation. He told me that he

(a) Corps Diplomatique anno 1664.

wished to preserve peace in Corsica. He had entered into
a convention with Paoli, mutually to give up such criminals as should fly into each others territories. Formerly
not one criminal in a hundred was punished. There was
no communication between the Corsicans and the Genoese;
and if a criminal could but escape from the one jurisdiction
to the other, he was safe. This was very easily done, so
that crimes from impunity were very frequent. By this
equitable convention, justice has been fully administered.

Perhaps indeed the residence of the French in Corsica,
has, upon the whole, been an advantage to the patriots.
There have been markets twice a week at the frontiers of
each garrison-town, where the Corsican peasants have
sold all sorts of provisions, and brought in a good many
French crowns; which have been melted down into
Corsican money. A cessation of arms for a few years
has been a breathing time to the nation, to prepare itself
for one great effort, which will probably end in the total
expulsion of the Genoese. A little leisure has been given
for attending to civil improvements, towards which the
example of the French has in no small degree contributed.
Many of the soldiers were excellent handy-craftsmen, and
could instruct the natives in various arts.

M. de Marboeuf entertained himself by laying out
several elegant pieces of pleasure ground; and such were
the humane and amicable dispositions of this respectable
officer, that he was at pains to observe what things were
most wanted in Corsica, and then imported them from
France, in order to shew an example to the inhabitants.
He introduced in particular, the culture of potatoes, of
which there were none in the island upon his arrival.
This root will be of considerable service to the Corsicans,
it will make a wholesome variety in their food; and as
there will thereby, of consequence, be less home con-

sumption of chestnuts, they will be able to export a greater quantity of them.

M. de Marboeuf made merry upon the reports which had been circulated, that I was no less than a minister from the British court. The Avignon Gazette brought us one day information, that the English were going to establish Un Bureau de Commerce in Corsica. 'O Sir, said he, the secret is out. I see now the motive of your destination to these parts. It is you who are to establish this Bureau de Commerce.'

Idle as these rumours were, it is a fact that, when I was at Genoa, Signor Gherardi, one of their secretaries of state, very seriously told me, 'Monsieur, vous m'avez fait trembler quoique je ne vous ai jamais vu. Sir, you have made me tremble although I never saw you before.' And when I smiled and assured him that I was just a simple traveller, he shook his head; but said, he had very authentick information concerning me. He then told me with great gravity, 'That while I travelled in Corsica, I was drest in scarlet and gold; but when I payed my respects to the Supreme Council at Corte, I appeared in a full suit of black.' These important truths I fairly owned to him, and he seemed to exult over me.

I was more and more obliged to M. de Marboeuf. When I was allowed by my physician, to go to his Excellency's table, where we had always a large company, and every thing in great magnificence, he was so careful of me, that he would not suffer me to eat any thing, or taste a glass of wine, more than was prescribed for me. He used to say, 'I am here both physician and commander in chief; so you must submit.' He very politely prest me to make some stay with him, saying, 'We have taken care of you when sick, I think we have a claim to you for a while, when in health.' His kindness followed me after I left him. It procured me an agreeable reception from M. Michel, the French chargé d'affaires at Genoa; and was the occasion of my being honoured with great civilities at Paris, by M. L'Abbé de Marboeuf conseiller d'etat, brother of the Count, and possessing similar virtues in private life.

I quitted Corsica with reluctance, when I thought of the illustrious Paoli. I wrote to him from Bastia, informing him of my illness, which I said, was owing to his having made me a man of so much consequence, that instead of putting me into a snug little room, he had lodged me in the magnificent old palace, where the wind and rain entered.

His answer to my first letter is written with so much spirit, that I begged his permission to publish it, which he granted in the genteelest manner, saying, ' I do not re- ' member the contents of the letter; but I have such a ' confidence in Mr. Boswell, that I am sure, he would not ' publish it, if there was any thing in it improper for ' publick view; so he has my permission.' I am thus enabled to present my readers with an original letter from Paoli.

To JAMES BOSWELL, Esq;
OF AUCHINLECK, SCOTLAND.

STIMATISSIMO SIGNOR BOSWELL,

RICEVEI la lettera che mi favori da Bastia, e mi consolo assai colla notizia di essersi rimessa in perfetta salute. Buon per lei che cadde in mano di un valente medico! Quando altra volta il disgusto de' paesi colti, ed ameni lo prendesse, e lo portasse in questa infelice contrada, procurerò che sia alloggiata in camere più calde, e custo- dita di quelle della casa Colonna in Sollacarò; mà ella ancora dovrà contentarsi di non viaggiare quando la giornata, e la stagione vogliono che si resti in casa per attendere il tempo buono. Io resto ora impaziente per la lettera che ha promesso scrivermi da Genova, dove dubito assai che la delicatezza di quelle dame non le abbia fatto fare qualche giorno di quarantena, per ispurgarsi di ogni anche più leggiero influsso, che possa avere portato seco dell' aria di questo paese; e molto più, se le fosse venuto il capriccio di far vedere quell' abito di veluto Corso, e quel berrettone, di cui i Corsi vogliono l'origine dagli elmi antichi, ed i Genovesi lo dicono inventato da quelli, che, rubando alla strada, non vogliano essere conosciuti; come se in tempo del loro governo avessero mai avuta apprensione di castigo i ladri pubblici? Son sicuro però, che ella presso avrà il buon partito con quelle amabili, e delicate persone, insinuando alle medesime, che il cuore delle belle è fatto per la compassione, non per il disprezzo, e per la tirannia; e cosi sarà rientrato facilmente nella lor grazia. Io ritornato in Corte ebbi subito la notizia del secreto sbarco dell' Abbatucci nelle spiaggie di Solenzara. Tutte le apparenze fanno credere che il medesimo sia venuto con disegni opposti alla pubblica quiete; pure si è constituito in castello, e protesta ravvedimento. Nel venire per Bocognano si seppe, che un capitano riformato Genovese cercava compagni per assassinarmi. Non potè rinvenirne e vedendosi scoperto si pose alla macchia, dove è stato ucciso dalle squadriglie che gli tenevano dietro i magistrati delle provincie oltramontane. Queste insidie non sembrano buoni preliminari del nostro accomodamento colla repubblica di Genova. Io sto passando il sindicato a questa provincia di Nebbio. Verso il 10 dell' entrante anderò per l'istesso oggetto in quella del Capocorso, ed il mese di Febrajo facilmente mi tratterrò in Balagna. Ritornerò poi in Corte alla primavera, per prepararmi all' apertura della consulta generale. In ogni luogo avrò presente la sua amicizia, e sarò desideroso de' continui suoi riscontri. Frattanto ella mi creda

Suo affettuosissimo amico

PATRIMONIO,
23 Decembre, 1765.

PASQUALE DE' PAOLI.

MUCH ESTEEMED MR. BOSWELL,

I RECEIVED the letter which you wrote to me from Bastia, and am much comforted by hearing that you are restored to perfect health. It is lucky for you that you fell into the hands of an able physician. When you shall again be seized with a disgust at improved and agreeable countries, and shall return to this ill-fated land, I will take care to have you lodged in warmer and better finished apartments than those of the house of Colonna, at Solla-carò. But you again should be satisfied not to travel when the weather and the season require one to keep within doors, and wait for a fair day. I expect with impatience the letter which you promised to write to me from Genoa, where I much suspect that the delicacy of the ladies will have obliged you to perform some days of quarantine, for purifying you from every the least infection, which you may have carried with you from the air of this country : and still more so, if you have taken the whim to shew that suit of Corsican velvet * and that bonnet of which the Corsicans will have the origin to be from the ancient helmets, whereas the Genoese say it was invented by those who rob on the high way, in order to disguise themselves ; as if during the Genoese government,

* By Corsican velvet he means the coarse stuff made in the island, which is all that the Corsicans have in stead of the fine velvet of Genoa.

publick robbers needed to fear punishment. I am sure however, that you will have taken the proper method with these amiable and delicate persons, insinuating to them, that the hearts of beauties are formed for compassion, and not for disdain and tyranny : and so you will have been easily restored to their good graces. Immediately on my return to Corte, I received information of the secret landing of Abbatucci (*a*), on the coast of Solenzara. All appearances make us believe, that he is come with designs contrary to the publick quiet. He has however surrendered himself a prisoner at the castle, and protests his repentance. As I passed by Bogognano, I learnt that a disbanded Genoese officer was seeking associates to assassinate me. He could not succeed, and finding that he was discovered, he betook himself to the woods; where he has been slain by the party detached by the magistrates of the provinces on the other side of the mountains, in order to intercept him. These ambuscades do not seem to be good preliminaries towards our accommodation with the republick of Genoa. I am now holding the syndicato in this province of Nebbio. About the 10th of next month, I shall go, for the same object, into the province of Capo Corso, and during the month of February, I shall probably fix my residence in Balagna. I shall return to Corte in the spring, to prepare myself for the opening of the General Consulta. Wherever I am, your friendship will be present to my mind, and I shall be desirous to continue a correspondence with you. Meanwhile believe me to be

Your most affectionate friend

PATRIMONIO,
23 December, 1765.

PASCAL PAOLI.

·  (*a*) Abbatucci, a Corsican of a very suspicious character.

Can any thing be more condescending, and at the same time shew more the firmness of an heroick mind, than this letter? With what a gallant pleasantry does the Corsican Chief talk of his enemies! One would think that the Queens of Genoa should become Rival Queens for Paoli. If they saw him, I am sure they would.

I take the liberty to repeat an observation made to me by that illustrious minister, whom Paoli calls the Pericles of Great Britain. ' It may be said of Paoli, as the Cardinal de Retz said of the great Montrose, " C'est un de ces hommes qu'on ne trouve plus que dans les Vies de Plutarque. He is one of those men who are no longer to be found but in the lives of Plutarch." '

THE END.

Pasquale Paoli (1725-1807)
b. Morosaglia, n.e. Corsica
exiled in Naples 1739-55
returned to Corsica in 1755
elected General of the Corsicans
established a constitution,
opened a university, etc,
ruled the island until the Genoese
with French assistance forced
Paoli into exile, in London, in 1769,
he returned to Corsica as
President, 1790-95; exiled again
to London where he died.

Printed in the United States
70952LV00001B/15

9 781885 586650